Empowering Your Life with MEDITATION

Empowering Your Life with MEDITATION

Delia Quigley

ALPHA

A member of Penguin Group (USA) Inc.

To my mother, Mary A. Quigley, who taught me
the meaning of following a spiritual path.

International Standard Book Number: 1-59257-268-5
Library of Congress Catalog Card Number: 2004106749

06   05   04   8   7   6   5   4   3   2   1

Interpretation of the printing code: The rightmost number of the first series of numbers is the year of the book's printing; the rightmost number of the second series of numbers is the number of the book's printing. For example, a printing code of 04-1 shows that the first printing occurred in 2004.

Printed in the United States of America

Publisher: Marie Butler-Knight

Product Manager: Phil Kitchel

Senior Managing Editor: Jennifer Chisholm

Acquisitions Editor: Mikal E. Belicove

Development Editor: Jennifer Moore

Production Editor: Megan Douglass

Copy Editor: Keith Cline

Cover Designer: Bill Thomas

Book Designer: Trina Wurst

Creative Director: Robin Lasek

Indexer: Angie Bess

Layout/Proofreading: Ayanna Lacey, Mary Hunt

iv

Contents

Introduction

When people ask me what I do for a living, I tell them I transform lives through the practice of meditation and yoga. Initially, they are usually skeptical, wondering how doing nothing (meditation) and exercising (yoga) can transform anything. Because words cannot replace the value of experience, I invite them to try it for themselves. In this book, I ask you to do the same.

I have taught meditation in church basements, bookstores, public schools and universities, martial arts dojos, neighborhood community centers, gymnasiums, spas, and yoga studios. Along the way, I have thought of myself as a Johnny Appleseed of meditation, dropping the seeds of transformation in fertile minds—always myself a student, however, having realized long ago that we teach what we most need to learn. The eight-limb path of Ashtanga yoga, which you will learn more about in Chapter 1, has guided me through the minefield of my emotions, memories, and rigid beliefs, step-by-sometimes-painful-step. I have learned not to expect anything but what each moment presents to me. I awaken each morning excited to do my meditation practice, eager to tap into the deep wellspring of my spiritual nature.

Whenever I start to feel overwhelmed by the problems of the world, I remind myself that the solution is very simple. It begins with sitting quietly and watching my breath. Yes, there's more, but that comes up while focusing on my breath and observing my mind as it dances like a drunken monkey. That *more* part is me; in your case, that *more* part is you.

As you establish a daily practice of meditation you will be pleasantly surprised to see the benefits show up in every area of your life. You will become a calmer, more focused individual or, as a student said to me, "I find that I am a nicer person than I was before." What she meant was that she had more patience with her children and colleagues. Her relationship with her husband has blossomed with understanding and acceptance that neither of them ever thought possible. Most of all she now savors the joy that happens with each spontaneous moment, knowing that it will go and return and go again. To live in the present moment is to live your life fully.

This is what you will come discover for yourself in *Empowering Your Life with Meditation:* how the practice of meditation is integral to understanding the consequences of your mind as it seeks permanence in an ever-changing world; how by sitting still you will discover your deeper spiritual nature; how you will know the cause of all suffering and how to bring it to an end. Pretty big claims to make, I agree, but I have been fortunate to experience these discoveries for myself and now have the great pleasure of sharing them with you.

All of the wonderful mental and physical benefits of meditation should be enough for any individual, but what follows this personal transformation is the clear understanding of our connection to other people, species, and nature. And this is how the world begins to shift toward peace and fellowship amongst all peoples.

As more and more students of meditation awaken to their inherent state of enlightenment, society inevitably moves along the same path. Those of us who meditate are part of what scholar and former Tibetan Buddhist monk Robert Thurman calls a cool revolution—one that reconstructs society by transforming each individual to a higher state of consciousness. Like any great movement, it takes time to grow, easing its way into the lives of people and opening their hearts to the possibility of world peace and the end to all suffering. Whereas political revolution constitutes a war for power, cool revolution happens within the individual. Transformation occurs on a spiritual level.

Impossible? Improbable? To that, I say, just begin. Take your time, read through this book, do the practice suggestions found in each chapter and keep a meditation journal to record your discoveries. There's really not much else to do, because just by practicing meditation your life will be profoundly and most positively transformed.

It is my great pleasure to share with you what I have learned on my spiritual journey. All that I ask is that you read the chapters and try the practice for yourself.

How to Use This Book

The chapters of this book are designed to guide you in beginning a practice of meditation and to help you see how it can transform 12 areas of your life. You will find tips, suggestions, and practical exercises to support you on your journey.

Each chapter ...

- Relates to a particular area of your life, such as work, love, and health, helping you to find your life's purpose.
- Contains stories from my own experience and those of my students and friends.
- Is interspersed with simple practices that allow you to better focus your mind.
- Concludes with guided and moving meditations and accompanying mantras to be used during your meditation practice.

It is best to read the first chapter, especially if you are just beginning a meditation practice. After you understand what meditation is about and how to sit for the first time, turn to a chapter that is of particular interest to you. This is a book that can be used throughout your lifetime. Your mind will always be plagued with thoughts and questions about your life. *Empowering Your Life with Meditation* provides you with the tools you need to sort through the chatter of your mind so you can find happiness and end suffering.

Welcome to the delightful and astounding path of meditation. Now let us begin from the beginning.

Acknowledgments

My grateful thanks to the wonderful editorial staff at Alpha books: Jennifer Moore, Megan Douglass, Keith Cline, and Mikal Belicove. Your guidance, suggestions, and patience were a great support.

To my agent Jacky Sach of Bookends, herself a dedicated meditator, my thanks for trusting me with seeing that the wisdom of meditation is shared with the world.

To my many friends, family, and students who appear on these pages, thank you for sharing your lives so that others may be liberated.

Most of all to the great teachers since before and after The Buddha, who have been the light for us all to follow, I thank you for your inspiration, kindness and courage.

Chapter 1

Choosing a Path of Meditation

"The ultimate goal of meditation is to experience the
full unfoldment of our own pure Consciousness,
the inner state of luminosity, love, and wisdom that
the Indian tradition calls the inner Self or the Heart."
—Sally Kempton

It's always best to know where you are going when setting
out on a long journey. So it is with learning to meditate. If
you have no idea why you are practicing to still the mind,
how will you know the next step, and the next? Take, for
instance, the story of the king who set out to meet his enemy.
He charged off to the east with a huge army of warriors
marching behind him. As they left the gates of the city, a
priest ran after them shouting, "Your Majesty, you must turn
your army around. You are going in the wrong direction!"

"What are you saying?" the king yelled back. "I have
thousands of men, war elephants, and guns all ready to go."

"Yes, your majesty," the priest replied, "but your army is
marching east and the enemy is encamped in the west! You're
moving in the wrong direction!"

You might do everything right in your meditation practice: wear the right clothing, have the right posture, breathe or recite your mantra properly, and be able to sit quietly for long hours and still your mind. But if you don't know where you are going—in other words, if you don't know the focus of your practice—you might find yourself in the king's shoes, traveling in the opposite direction of where you want to go.

So why meditate? The ultimate goal of meditation is to come to know the nature of Self. Maybe you call it self-actualization. If you are a Christian, you might call it the Holy Spirit within. A Buddhist knows this as Buddha nature. No matter what you call it, your true Self—I will refer to it throughout this book with a capital S—has always been there. It is you. However, it has become obscured by the veil of illusion through which you see the world.

Let Your Light Shine Through

This morning I awoke to find my windows covered with frost from the winter's cold. The rising sun was a pale ghost of light trying to come through the icy glass, and I thought, this is how our true Self is obscured from our sight. Distracted by the intricate patterns made by the ice, I invented castles, faces, mountain ranges, and snowflakes. Because it was such a faint glow off in the distance, I ignored the light. As the morning progressed, the sun melted the frost and little by little revealed to me her brilliance. For meditation to reveal the nature of Self, you must first melt the veil of illusion, distortion, and mental affliction that clouds your mind and allow the light of your true Self to manifest fully.

The History of Meditation

"The devil is that aspect of ourselves that is unexplored, unac-knowledged, denied, pushed out. Mara it is called in Sanskrit."

—Ven. Traleg Khyabgon Rinpoche

From historical research, we know that the practice of meditation flourished long before the birth of the man who went on to become Lord Buddha. In the Indus Valley, from 2800 to 1800 B.C.E., there existed a highly advanced, agrarian society that practiced meditation and yoga. So although the Buddha was not the first human to become enlightened, nor the last, he was the first to create a path that others could follow to enlightenment.

The Story of Prince Siddhartha

Prince Siddhartha Gotama Shakyamuni, known today as Shakyamuni, the Sage of the Shakya Clan, or Lord Buddha, the Blessed One, was born 2,500 years ago into a life of luxury and privilege as the son of a king in Lumbini, Nepal. Before his birth, seers came to his father and predicted that his newborn child would be a great king or an enlightened one. The king, eager for Gotama to follow him onto the throne, kept the boy sheltered within the palace walls and away from the distractions of the outside world. Gotama grew up well cared for by his parents and the people around him, married a woman he loved, and fathered a son.

At the age of 29 years, Gotama took his wife and a party of friends for an outing outside the walls of the palace. When he encountered sickness, old age, and death among the people, he was stunned and moved to compassion. Determined to find a way to bring about an end to the suffering of all beings, he left his family and his life of ease and took on the life of an ascetic monk.

Over the next six years Gotama studied one practice after another, seeking the way to liberation and true bliss. During a period of severe asceticism, starved and too weak to maintain his health, he heard a boatman on the river instruct a young musician how to tune the strings of his instrument. The boatman told the musician that if the string is too tight it will break from the tension and if it is to loose it will not play the proper note. The middle way, the boatman advised, is the right strength for the string to be tuned. Upon hearing this advice, Gotama knew that his severe lifestyle was only destroying him and, with that, he abandoned his ascetic path and followed a more moderate one—a middle way—allowing himself food and drink.

Not long after his change in lifestyle, Gotama came to a place in northern India called Bodhgaya and sat down under a Bodhi tree, determined not to rise until he had gained enlightenment and found the truth of existence. It was in this meditation that he was visited by the Mara, a devil, who had come to distract him and drive him from his purpose.

First the Mara showed him a vision of mass destruction, but he did not move from his place. Then it tempted him with the vision of beautiful women, but he stayed in meditation and was not distracted. At the last the Mara fired arrows at him, but before reaching him the weapons turned to flowers and fell at his feet. Having defeated the power of the Mara, the veil of illusion lifted and he became a fully enlightened Buddha—the awakened one—embodying all the positive qualities of a sentient being and releasing himself of all the negative aspects.

In his enlightened or awakened state, Shakyamuni Buddha realized the true nature of existence and discovered the path toward ending all suffering. With a nod to the Indus Valley tradition that preceded him, he pointed out that his was an ancient path, and on this path the refinement of one's mental development is as important as maintaining a practice of meditation.

The Buddha's life is an example of how a certain amount of hardship is necessary when walking down a spiritual path. It is only through dedicated perseverance and a commitment to daily practice that one can achieve the ultimate awakening or liberation from suffering. This is not something you can buy for yourself, or have someone else practice for you; nor can you predict when the awakening will happen. It's best to give up any attachments to time, and to results of any kind, for that matter. Just sit, do nothing, and let the practice change you.

The Four Noble Truths

"I teach about suffering and the way to end it."
—Shakyamuni Buddha

Seven weeks after attaining enlightenment, the Buddha gave his first sermon on what he had realized. He called his teachings the Four Noble Truths. These four truths constitute the essence of the Buddhist path— or any meditation practice, for that matter—regardless of the tradition one follows, since what the Buddha describes is the very nature of being human. The Four Noble Truths are guidelines to use on your path toward the realization that you are already enlightened but that you cannot see past the veil of illusion that you create— you see and hear only what you want to see and hear. Applying the Buddha's teachings can help clear the way of all your mental wanderings, bringing more clarity and understanding to your life.

The Truth of Suffering

Although we would like to be happy and wish happiness for others, nonetheless, our nature is to suffer and to cause others to suffer. The Buddhist defines "suffering" not just as a physical pain of the body, but also the discontent our minds are afflicted with most of our waking day. For many people, this truth sounds extreme or even contradictory. How can the essence of life be suffering, when we also sometimes feel great happiness—even so joyful that we believe life couldn't get any better?

Buddhist teacher and scholar Bhante Henepola Gunaratana addresses the conflict between our occasional feelings of joy and the truth of suffering. In *Mindfulness in Plain English,* he asks that you take any moment when you feel fulfilled and examine it closely. You will find that down under the joy there is a subtle undercurrent of tension, the knowledge that no matter how great the moment is, it is going to end. No matter how much you just gained, you are either going to lose some of it or spend the rest of your days guarding what you have got and scheming how to get more. And in the end, you are going to die. In the end, you lose everything. It is all transitory. Happiness and suffering are a natural part of the human condition. To find a better way of being in the world, we must first find the cause of our suffering.

The Truth of the Cause of Suffering

"Suffering is nothing but existence enslaved to ignorance."
—The Dalai Lama

Our suffering arises from the afflictions of our mind, the result of the negative emotions—attachment, greed, jealousy, pride, anger, and hatred—that run our lives. This originates from our feeling of separation from each other, our idea that we are the center of a universe created to serve our every whim and need. This separation creates a downward spiral of emotions that leads to isolation and the need to fill our empty lives with possessions and friends and partners, none of whom can satisfy the vastness of our loneliness.

The Little Sufferings

You might have felt great when you woke up this morning, but as the day progressed many small incidents began to cloud your initial joy. Maybe it started when you got dressed and discovered your pants were a bit too tight; you had gained a few pounds and felt guilty about eating too much. Then you opened up your credit card bill and were shocked to see how much—most of it stuff you didn't need—you had bought this past month. By now you're agitated, and the joy you felt earlier in the day has been replaced with negative thoughts. This is the mental suffering that returns time and again to block out the feelings of happiness. Not necessarily huge, tragic events, but a consistent barrage of complaints about the world around us.

The Truth of the Cessation of Suffering

"Enlightenment—that magnificent escape from anguish and ignorance—never happens by accident. It results from the brave and sometimes lonely battle of one person against his own weaknesses."

—Bhikkhu Nyanasobhano

When we confront the truth—that the essence of life is suffering—and recognize the cause of that suffering—our negative feelings, our separation from one another, and our belief that we are the center of the universe—we can take the appropriate steps to end the suffering. We do this by freeing ourselves from the dependent states of our mind. The Buddha freed himself through meditation and following the middle way. We, too, can liberate ourselves from the endless cycle of being run by our delusions about how our life should unfold.

The Truth of The Eightfold Noble Path

"Share your love, your wisdom, and your wealth and serve each other as much as possible. Live in harmony with one another and be an example of peace, love, compassion, and wisdom."

—Lama Thubten Yeshe

Meditation is a powerful tool we can use to attain freedom from the habits of our minds. However, this liberation doesn't happen overnight, nor does it happen just because we sit in silence and observe our thoughts. There is homework to be done and actions to be carried over into our everyday lives, including our relationships with others.

The Buddha was very specific in his teachings as to the correct attitude and actions we should all follow as we strive for liberation. He recommended the following eight attitudes and actions, often referred to as the eightfold noble path:

- **Correct thought.** Avoid covetousness, the wish to harm others, and wrong views.
- **Correct speech.** Avoid lying, divisive and harsh speech, and idle gossip.
- **Correct actions.** Avoid killing, stealing, and sexual misconduct.
- **Correct livelihood.** Avoid work that causes harm to yourself, others, and the environment. This entails correct thought, correct speech, and correct actions.
- **Correct understanding.** Develop genuine wisdom.
- **Correct effort.** Take each step with joyful perseverance.
- **Correct mindfulness.** Live in the present, instead of dreaming of the future.
- **Correct concentration.** Keep a steady, calm, and attentive state of mind.

You will recognize the Noble Truths in a number of forms throughout the chapters of this book. The many traditions of meditation all acknowledge that "right" behavior aligns with a spiritual practice. You will see this in the teachings of Patanjali's yoga sutras, the holy scripture, the Bhagavad Gita, the teachings of J. Krishnamurti, and the many other styles of meditation.

The Source of All Happiness

"The more compassionate you are, the more generous you can be. The more generous you are, the more loving friendliness you cultivate to help the world."
—Thich Nhat Hanh

The essence of the Buddha's teachings is how to end our suffering and find true happiness. The path toward this goal is to practice meditation. To achieve the state of buddhahood, you must practice compassion, the root of the Buddha's teachings. You must awaken the mind of Bodhichitta, an altruistic wish to achieve buddhahood for the sake of all sentient beings. And you must have the skilful means to make sure you are practicing correctly.

Practicing meditation can bring you a short-term happiness that consists of physical and mental pleasure. However, the root of maintaining these experiences is with a mind that is at peace, a mind that is free of suffering.

If your mind is unhappy and in constant turmoil from the mental afflictions, then regardless of how great the physical pleasure may be it will not take the form of happiness. It will merely be a transitory grasping for something to dispel your fear and fill the internal emptiness. If, on the other hand, you merely lack the ideal physical pleasures and the material ideals of wealth but your mind is at peace, you will be happy.

Types of Meditation: Which Path to Choose

"Journey of a thousand miles, begins with first step."
—Confucius

Ultimately, meditation brings you the awareness of what some call God, others call Divine Spirit, and still others refer to as one's Higher Self. In the five practices that I describe in this section, you will see how they all involve a different study, yet follow a similar path. Regardless of your religious belief, the practice of meditation will only improve and enhance every area of your life.

Beginning with the Buddha, those teachers and students who have gone before have marked the path with words of encouragement and advice and with their own actions for those who wish to follow. No matter which path you decide to take, what it comes down to is sitting quietly in silence, whether in a group of other spiritual-minded individuals or alone, and allowing the time to dissolve while you do nothing.

The study of meditation is not limited to the five practices I have chosen to describe in this chapter. However, these will give you a place from which to step off onto the path. Look over the descriptions that follow and choose one that speaks to your heart, locate your local meditation and yoga schools, pick up the telephone, and begin your journey.

Buddhist Insight Meditation

"Wherever you go, there you are."

—Jon Kabat-Zinn

Your mind is going a mile a minute trying to comprehend the events of your day, making it very difficult to focus on any one thing. You've heard that meditation is about learning to concentrate your mind and clear away all your thoughts, but it seems impossible to do that when you can't find the off switch that will quiet the chatter. Insight meditation seeks the real nature of the world as it is, free of our imposed and rationalized concepts. It teaches you to appreciate that *this* is the only moment of your life: The past is gone, and the future has yet to unfold. The way to find the true nature of the world is through the practice of mindfulness—in meditation and in all other areas of your life. It is not sufficient just to concentrate on a word, image, or thought, but to embody the essence of the moment. In other words, concentration pins the mind to its object, whereas it is mindfulness that carefully and thoroughly gets a good look at it. When you have found out what that thing really is, you have developed wisdom. This wisdom brings awareness of the impermanence of all things, thereby releasing you from the affliction of constant attachment to outcome, desire, pleasure, and thinking you are right.

When practicing insight meditation, you observe everything with concentrated awareness. You experience the rising and falling of your abdomen, your buttocks and legs sitting and touching the floor and cushion, any pain in the body, feet falling asleep, and thoughts,

thoughts, and more thoughts. As you sit, you will soon discover that all you observe—your physical sensations, emotions, and thoughts—are just processes that arise and pass away rapidly. You begin to realize that these processes are impermanent, constantly changing, and beyond your control. With this insight you are able to abandon your "false self"—that image you have of yourself influenced by what has been said and experienced from your past—and finally return to the pure enlightened mind which is your original nature.

When you understand what constitutes mindfulness, you can be mindful during all your activities. It will begin from the moment you wake up in the morning, as you notice your eyes opening. With this same state of mindfulness, you will wash, eat, drive, laugh, speak, and so on, throughout the day. You will be ever present to the immediate moment while it is happening.

Ashtanga: The Eight Limbs of Yoga

"The eight limbs of yoga are: respect toward others, self-restraint, posture, breath control, detaching at will from the senses, concentration, meditation, and contemplation."
—Patanjali, Yoga Sutra II.29

From its humble beginnings in India thousands of years ago, yoga has spread worldwide and today is practiced in gyms, corporate office buildings, church basements, as well as yoga studios. The Yoga Sutras are the "bible" of the practice, and although the exact historical date is in doubt, it is said that they were written more than 5,000 years ago by the sage Patanjali. The original and only intent of Ashtanga yoga is to liberate the mind through meditation and thus awaken to our true enlightened nature.

Of the 196 aphorisms, or principles, that make up the Yoga Sutras, Patanjali dedicated three for asana (postures), seven for pranayama (breath), and the remaining 186 instruct the student in the understanding and mastery over the mind through the practice of meditation. Although Ashtanga yoga encompasses eight "limbs" or steps, many people are only familiar with the third limb—asana, also called Hatha yoga. The more than 1,000 *asanas*, or postures, are designed to stretch and tone every muscle in the body. This is the aspect of yoga that predominates in the western world.

The eight "limbs" are as follows:

1. *The Yamas.* Follow the five restraints, or correct methods of attitude, known as the *Yamas.* The Yamas are nonharming, honesty, nonstealing, moderation, and generosity.

2. *The Niyamas.* Fill your daily living with consciousness of the five *Niyamas,* or observances. The Niyamas are commitment, contentment, passion, self-awareness, and selfless devotion to God.

3. *Asana.* Stretch and strengthen your body with specific postures. These positions not only lengthen tight hamstrings and ease the stress in your back and shoulders, but also work to focus and quiet your mind.

4. *Pranayama.* Here the focus is on the flow of your breath, directing your mind to the life force, *prana,* which sets your mind free from its restrictive chatter.

5. *Pratyahara.* Withdraw your senses, sight, sound, taste, touch, and smell, inward toward the center of your being and bring your focus to one point. (Both *Asana* and *Pranayama* are means to achieving *Pratyahara.*)

6. *Dharana.* Taking yourself deeper into a state of meditative absorption, begin to concentrate without distraction from mental chatter.

7. *Dhyana.* After releasing the tensions and limitation from the body and learning to focus and then concentrate the mind, you are finally ready to be absorbed in meditation.

8. *Samadhi.* The final liberation of the mind into superconsciousness and blissful union with the mystery body known as Divine Love.

The eight limb path of yoga is a step-by-step progression that can span a lifetime of study and contemplation. I follow the eight limb path of yoga, and it informs much of what I have to say about meditation in this book. I have attempted to balance this information with teachings from several schools of Buddhism, contemporary works by New Age teachers, as well as the Christian perspective of meditation. My aim is to give you as broad a view as possible in which to begin your study of meditation.

Zen Buddhist Meditation

"In the beginner's mind there are many possibilities, but in the expert's there are few."

—Shunryu Suzuki

The path we step onto when we are born into this lifetime can be winding and perilous when viewed with our ego-identified mind. We base our actions on surviving in a world fraught with danger, with no one we can truly trust. All this work and effort to "be someone" and to accomplish something, and then we die ... just like that, we die. So what was all that pain and struggle really about? In Zen teachings, it is all about self-realization. It is about human beings awakening to what is real in the world and what is illusion. It is also about seeing how your fears and negative emotions are run by your ego-identified mind and how to move past them to an empty mind. When your mind is empty it is open to receive and learn, it is ready for anything.

Zen Buddhism originated in China sometime during the sixth century. The Chinese name for this path of meditation is called *Ch'an*, which stems from the Sanskrit word *dhyan*, which means "meditation." When the practice was brought to Japan, it was translated as *Zen*, and retains this name to the present day. The Zen practice of meditation brings you into the here and now, where you see that the past is a finished chapter and the future is yet to be created. In your daily existence, you are continually asked to identify yourself as being someone; I am a mother, I am a teacher, I am a doctor, but these "labels" we create for ourselves are irrelevant. Our identification with these images of our self only serves to hold us back from seeing who we truly are. In the Zen practice of meditation, time, labels, and space all fall away leaving you with a pure, calm mind where there is no 'I', no world, no body, no mind.

Beginners Welcome

Zen meditation asks that you come to your meditation practice with a beginner's mind so that there is space for you to learn. Shunryu Suzuki, in *Zen Mind, Beginner's Mind*, tells us that the beginner should have no thought of having attained something. When we have no thought of achievement, no thought of self, there is space for us to learn. The empty mind is one of compassion. When our mind is compassionate, it is boundless.

The sitting practice of Zen meditation is called *zazen* and refers to the meditation position: sitting on a cushion, hands resting one atop the other with thumbs touching, eyes closed, thoughts focused on the breath. No words can convey what happens when you are absorbed in a meditative moment. If you were to observe a room full of people sitting on their cushions meditating, it would look like nothing was happening, yet within each one of those individual minds there would be a wide range of activity taking place.

Zen meditation should be practiced daily, beginning with 5 to 10 minutes and building up to one hour. Groups of meditators gather together during the week or weekend for half and full day sessions, and also 5 to 10 day meditation retreats throughout the year.

A monk once asked his master, "No matter what lies ahead, what is the Way?" The master quickly replied, "The Way is your daily life." This concept is at the very heart of the way of Zen.

Transcendental Meditation

Transcendental meditation was developed by the Maharishi Mahesh Yogi, to accommodate the Western lifestyle and mentality. It is said to be a simple and easily learned mental technique. There is no manipulation or suggestion, such as in hypnosis, nor does it require the ability to concentrate or control the mind. It requires no physical exercises, special postures, or procedures. Transcendental meditation is practiced for 15 to 20 minutes: once in the morning before breakfast, to start the day with alertness and energy, and once again in the afternoon before dinner. You can practice the technique anywhere—in your office after work, riding the subway, sitting in a plane, or even in your car parked at a highway rest stop; but it is usually practiced in the comfort of your own home.

During transcendental meditation, the mind settles down to a silent, yet fully awake, state of awareness—pure consciousness. Pure consciousness is the source of the unlimited creativity and intelligence of the mind. At the same time, the body gains a unique and profound state of rest and relaxation. Research has shown that the twice-daily experience of pure consciousness during transcendental meditation makes the mind more alert, creative, and intelligent throughout the day. And the deep rest provided by transcendental meditation eliminates the buildup of stress and tension; improves health; and provides the basis for more dynamic, productive, and satisfying activity.

Christian Meditation

In Christian meditation, the purpose is not to still the mind, but to awaken communication with God in the form of contemplative prayer. In this way meditation and prayer work together to direct one's thoughts and intentions to a higher spiritual connection. Deeper than all ideas of God is God himself. Deeper than imagination is the reality of God. Thus, in this way of "pure prayer," you leave all thoughts, words, and images behind in order to "set your mind on the kingdom of God before all else." In this way, you leave your egotistical self behind to die and rise to your true self in Christ.

Practitioners of Christian meditation undertake an inner journey of silence, stillness, and simplicity. They embrace poverty of spirit, a radical letting-go of all distractions, including all thoughts, words, and images. One takes a single sacred word or phrase (a *mantra*) or a short prayer and simply and faithfully repeats it during the period of meditation. Two periods of meditation of about 20 to 30 minutes are advisable, at the beginning and end of each day. A quiet time and place, an upright posture, fidelity, and perseverance are the only requirements.

Christian meditation is unfamiliar to many devout Christians, despite its ancient place in Christian tradition. Alone or combined with prayer, meditation allows you to recognize the seeds of contemplation within yourself. Through meditation you come to acknowledge the potential of the "holiness of all the people of God."

Most Christian meditation groups today are led by lay people. In this renewal of a Christian tradition of prayer, there is also great potential for Christians of all denominations to meet in common faith, and indeed, for all people of all faiths to meet in their common humanity.

A Journey of Discovery

When looking at the different paths of meditation you may well wonder whether if one path is any better than another. That is for you to discover for yourself as you make the journey. What you will find along the way might surprise, confuse, free, and delight you. You might also experience fright, frustration, depression, and anger. You most definitely will meet yourself head-on and get to hear what your ego has to say about that. Mental afflictions will rise up to claim every attempt you make at right thinking, and you will cave in, over and over again, considering at times that meditation is much too difficult and that you will never get the hang of it. However, as your practice teaches you to be patient, you will come to see the many benefits of sitting quietly and doing nothing.

Preparing the Body for Meditation

"Meditation is an effort in the beginning. Later on it becomes habitual and gives bliss, joy, and peace."

—Swami Sivananda

You should now have a basic understanding of five different types of meditation. You may want to explore them, one at a time, by reading books or searching various websites (see Appendix B). In doing so, you will come to find a style of meditation that inspires you to learn more. If you are ready to get started, the following steps will help you prepare for your practice.

Creating Your Sacred Space

Choose somewhere in your home where you won't be disturbed. This can be a corner of your bedroom, a closet, a part of your living room—anywhere you can set up an altar and sit comfortably. Make this a place where you will come to practice at the same time each day. Cover a table with cloth, and arrange some candles, incense, and, if you like, a picture of Buddha or another religious icon of your choosing. Purchase a meditation cushion or simply use a comfortable pillow. If you prefer, a straight-backed chair will work fine.

Finding a Comfortable Posture

It is important to be as comfortable as possible during your meditation practice. If you sit on the floor, use a cushion and cross your legs, Indian style, with your knees resting on the floor.

You can also sit in a chair with both feet planted firmly on the floor with your back straight and supported. Or you can sit with your back against a wall for support, or even sit upright with the support coming from your body's own strength. The point is to keep the spine straight and naturally aligned, with the weight of the body distributed around it in a balanced pattern. In this way, gravity, not muscular tension, is the primary stabilizing influence. The right attitude for meditation can itself be described as poised: alert yet also relaxed. Poised posture promotes the right state of attention-awareness for successful meditation.

Lay down on your back only if you are able to stay awake during meditation. For many people, the pull to doze is too seductive. It might help to keep your body slightly elevated on a slant—lying on the couch with a pillow supporting your shoulders, for instance. If you don't nap during the day, you probably can work from this position.

Concentrating on Your Breath

Concentrating on your breath helps train the mind to be still. Inhale and exhale through your nose, moving naturally with the rise and fall of your diaphragm.

Try counting to 10 in this way: *Breath in, breath out, one. Breath in, breath out, two. Breath in, breath out, three.* You may never get to five because you'll have remembered something you had to do, the line from a song, a memory of long ago, and then, oh, yeah, the breath. Start again. *Breath in, breath out, one.* Don't worry about stopping the thoughts, just keep bringing your focus back to counting each inhale and exhale.

As you attempt to stay focused on your breath you will find your mind wandering constantly. This is normal, but whenever you catch yourself doing it, bring your awareness back to your breath. With practice, you will be able to maintain your focus for longer periods of time.

Choosing a Mantra or Other Focus Technique

You might find that after a few minutes of meditation your body is sitting still, but your mind is running like a faucet turned full on. You may want to use a *mantra* to help keep your mind focused on one thing at a time.

A *mantra* is a word or phrase that helps you to focus your mind and quiet other distracting thoughts. They are used throughout this book to help lead you into a deeper stillness while calming your mind. If there is a particular word that helps you to relax and calm your thoughts then try repeating it over and over in your mind. For instance, in Yoga meditation, the mantra used is usually a Sanskrit word or syllable such as OM. OM is the original mantra, the root of all sounds and letters, and thus of all language and thought. The "O" is sounded deep within the body, and slowly brought upward joining with the "M," which then resonates through the entire head. Repeating OM for 20 minutes relaxes every atom in your body.

Techniques that use a repetitive sound or phrase, prayer, or mantra have been found to bring forth positive physiological changes. Maharishi Mahesh Yogi says that the thought-sound of a mantra takes the meditator to the source of his or her thought. Studies of the brainwave patterns of meditators indicate that the deepest relaxation results when thoughts are few or absent.

In Buddhism, instead of a mantra, you focus on your breathing. Both mantras and concentrated breathing help to create a state of relaxation. If you make awareness of breathing your single meditation method, let your attention dwell on the gentle rise and fall of your abdomen as you breathe in and out. Your breathing will become very quiet, and after several minutes of meditation the gentle movement and rhythm of your breathing will relax you.

Some meditation methods involve looking at objects with open eyes, whereas in others, the subjects close their eyes.

Dressing for Meditation

Wear clothes that are loose and comfortable—tight or ill-fitting clothes will be distracting. Wear socks if you tend to get cold feet, but remove your shoes for the actual sitting time. Pay attention to the temperature in the room so that you dress in such a way that you don't have to add or remove layers during your practice. Consider keeping a prayer shawl or light blanket nearby, which you can drape over your shoulders to keep you warm if necessary.

Keeping a Meditation Journal

It's a good idea to keep a journal and record your insights from your meditation practice. A simple notebook will work, but use it solely for meditation. In some chapters I ask you to make certain observations and note them in your journal. You can refer back to what you have written to view your progress or to better understand a particular thought or insight you had. Try to make a habit of writing a few lines after each sitting to see what, in particular, came up in your thoughts that day.

Moving Meditation: Do-In and Stretching

Each chapter in this book concludes with both a moving and a guided meditation. The moving meditation will involve some kind of physical activity designed to bring you to a deeper awareness of a particular area of your life. It requires that you give to it the same quality of awareness you would sitting quietly in contemplation. Each guided meditation will take you through specific meditative lessons to help concentrate your mind and bring you to a deeper understanding of yourself.

The Japanese body massage technique called *Do-In,* which involves "hammering" your body with your hands (trust me, it feels good), is an excellent way to stimulate the flow of energy throughout your entire body. Combining *Do-In* with stretches prepares your body for meditating by helping to release stress and tension, lengthening the muscles, stimulating the flow of energy, and opening your lungs.

The Body Stretch

Stand comfortably with your two feet a hand's distance apart and parallel to each other. On an inhale of breath, bring your arms overhead, in front of your face, and look up toward your fingers. As you exhale, lower your arms slowly, bend your knees, and round your back as you attempt to touch your fingertips to the floor. On the next inhale, begin to round back up to a straight position, bringing your head up last. Exhale while standing, and then begin again on the inhale.

Time each movement to the length of each breath. Let your body do the breathing while you observe and follow. Make sure that as soon as the inhale is complete you move right into the exhale, without holding your breath. Your movements should always *follow* your breath. Repeat this movement five times, and then stand with your body erect, close your eyes, and make a mental note of how your body is feeling.

Do-In

Next, open your eyes, extend your left arm, and with your right hand in a fist gently punch the left hand moving up the inside of the arm and down the outside, then up the front of the left arm across your chest. Now change hands and use the left fist to punch down the inside of the right arm and up the outside. Using both fists, gently punch the chest area (remember Tarzan?), working around your breasts in a clockwise direction, down your sides to the lower belly, moving again in a clockwise direction to stimulate the lower intestines.

Continue punching gently down the outside of your legs (right hand/right leg, left hand/left leg) coming up the inside to the groin (careful here), and then down the front of each leg and up the back where you can pummel your derriere (buttocks) with a bit more enthusiasm, softening on the lower back. When this is complete, bring yourself upright and use your fists to lightly hammer the back of your shoulders, up the back of your neck, and over and around your head. Massage your forehead, cheeks, jaw, temples, and finish with a light tapping of your fingers on the face. Bring your arms down to your sides, stand quietly, close your eyes, and focus on your breath. Notice how your body feels after the stretch and energy massage.

Release Mantra

As you are stretching and hammering on yourself, recite the following mantra, called a release mantra:

Stretching my body I release old tension.

Using my hands I charge my body with energy.

With each breath I feed myself love.

Recite one or all three lines, depending on how many of them you remember. This helps to create a stronger body/mind/breath connection.

The stretching and hammering should take you about five minutes to complete, depending on how slowly you perform the exercises. Now take your seat on the cushion or chair, and let's begin your meditation.

Guided Meditation: Classic Beginners Meditation

You can set a quiet timer to go off after 5 to 10 minutes, if you are concerned about how much time has passed during your practice. This way your thoughts won't be distracted with this additional concern.

Begin by sitting quietly with your hands placed on your thighs, elbows bent, arms relaxed. Allow your body to find its upright posture without forcing or exaggerating the position. Release any tension in your shoulders, jaw, and facial muscles.

Bring your full attention to the exhale of breath through your nose. Without forcing or attempting to breath, allow yourself to observe the flow of breath as it leaves your body. Recite the beginner's mantra (coming up next) silently with each inhale and exhale. Thoughts will continue to distract you from your focus, so when this happens just—note mentally, "oops, I'm thinking"—and then return to the mantra.

While in meditation, remain still. When you experience physical discomfort from your position, try not to move. Ignore it if it is minor; if it stands out and grabs your attention, however, you will have to make it your main subject of observation. View any dark emotions as clouds passing across a calm, blue sky. With practice, the mind will wander less and stay with the mantra and the rise and fall of the breath. Complete the session when the timer goes off.

Beginner's Mantra

Breathing in.

Breathing out.

Although it may seem simple and easy to do, after you have experienced this short practice you will understand how difficult it is to sit and do nothing. Be patient, follow this and the other practices in the book, and observe the transformation that takes place.

Chapter 2

Enriched Spirituality

Spirituality is the path of communion with a higher, greater power than our human self. This is our small self—I'll refer to it with a lowercase "s" throughout—the one trapped by the illusions, stories, and dramas we create with our mind. What we are seeking is to elevate our consciousness and connect to our higher true Self, which is within us waiting to be set free.

The spiritual guru Swami Muktananda taught that within every person there is this *Shakti,* meaning the divine power, God's power. And it is only because of this power that we live. This power is also known as the Self, or God. As long as you do not know the Self, no matter how much you try to improve on the outside, you cannot really improve.

Throughout the chapters of this book I will refer to this higher state of consciousness by different names, just as you might in your spiritual practice. They are not used in connection with any one religious practice, but are directed toward the understanding that the great mystery of life and this universe lies within the power of what are called ...

- God or Goddess
- Divine Spirit
- Higher Power
- Higher Self
- Higher Consciousness

It is the nature of humans to constantly seek something that will make sense of their lives and give them a reason for living. For thousands of years, religion has fed this need with the image of an all-powerful God to which we pray for guidance and mercy. However, the all-too-human conduct of gurus, priests, and other religious leaders has caused many people, like yourself, to reconsider the role of religion in your life. In place of religion, many have turned to meditation, where they find the quiet and peace necessary to hear the voice of the Divine Spirit within.

Whether or not you begin a meditation practice to become more spiritual, at some point you might encounter certain feelings and experiences that lead you to recognize the spiritual path you have stepped on. As I have said, these experiences will be different for each individual and should not be compared or judged by what has happened to others. In the course of your practice you may experience ...

- Feelings of joy and well-being.
- Colored lights, sounds, or shapes that have a spiritual connection.
- A feeling of being connected to all there is in the world.
- A dropping away of your body and mind, leaving you in a space of pure awareness.
- The knowledge that there is a sacred presence deep within you.
- Feelings of love for others, while feeling truly loved by God.
- An awareness of spiritual beings and angels in your presence.

Whereas following the tenets of a structured religion is to walk a spiritual path for many people, there are equally as many individuals who choose to find their own way. What they all have in common is the innate understanding that there is something extraordinary that calls us to grow as compassionate and loving human beings.

Your meditation practice will take you step-by-step, allowing you to make progress at your pace, at your level of understanding. It will open you to the discovery that you are intimately connected to all of creation, and it will guide you to find your true Self. As you learned in Chapter 1, there are many paths you can take—among them Buddhist meditation, yoga, transcendental meditation, and Christian meditation—to get beyond the false veil of reality to find your true nature. All of the paths involve awakening yourself to your full potential as a loving and compassionate being.

Looking Within for Divine Presence

"Why are you wandering? All is within. Go and sit at home. What is there outside?"

—Swami Nityananda

One day you wake up and see that something is missing in your life despite having three cars, a large house, a husband, wife, lover, and children. You begin to question and search, hungry for some kind of spiritual fulfillment. You set off on a journey to find a teacher, or you turn to the church looking for God. You open the Bible, the Bhagavad-Gita, Patanjali's Sutras, the gospels of Jesus, and they all say to seek the answer within. Although they may agree on many points, these ancient teachings also have their own unique way of viewing our human place in the world. These can include the idea that:

- You are perfection already.
- To see yourself as inferior, unworthy, and trapped in a life of suffering is to miss the joy that awaits your discovery.
- You must put an end to seeing yourself as a limited being.
- Meditate to anchor yourself in the sense of your unlimited ability, greatness, and purity.
- You suffer because you have separated yourself from the One source, that is God.

Buddhist Spiritual Teachings

Since many of the teachings about meditation come to us from the life of Shakyamuni Buddha I include here three important Buddhist concepts to consider that pertain to the study of meditation:

- *Karma.* This refers to the law of cause and effect in a person's life. In a nutshell, karma means that you reap what you have sown. According to the law of karma, you are who you are and what you do as a result of your actions in previous lifetimes (more on the Buddhist philosophy of life and rebirth in the next paragraph). The life you are now leading was the inevitable outcome of what you were and did in still earlier incarnations. Your reincarnation in the next life depends on your actions in this present life.

- *Samsara.* The cycle of birth, death, and rebirth. This is called "the wheel of samsara." The Buddha taught that the existence of an individual self or ego is an illusion. There is no eternal substance of a person that goes through the rebirth cycle. What goes through the rebirth cycle is only a set of feelings, impressions, present moments, and one's karma. In other words, as one lifetime ends and you reincarnate, your human personality in one existence is the direct cause of your individuality in the next. The new individual in the next life will not be exactly the same person, but there will be several similarities.

- *Nirvana.* Not to be confused with the Christian idea of a heaven, nirvana means "the blowing out" of existence. It is an eternal state of being. Here is where the karma and samsara are complete. All suffering ends, meaning that you've reached a state where there are no desires and the individual consciousness ceases to be. The Buddha taught that "there is a condition, where there is neither earth nor water, neither air nor light, neither limitless space, nor limitless time, neither any kind of being, neither ideation nor non-ideation, neither this world nor that world. There is neither arising nor passing away, nor dying, neither cause nor effect, neither change nor standstill." The state of nirvana is a state of formless consciousness.

Take a deep breath and go back and read that again. As I said before, words cannot adequately convey the picture, so to read about "formless consciousness" with some understanding is impossible without the personal experience. So relax if you are having a difficult time grasping the concepts. At this point, all you need to know is that our spiritual identity exists in the plane of form and matter, while there is a separate plane in which pure spirit resides.

Seeking Enlightenment

The Buddha passed on his experience of enlightenment in teachings of meditation that basically say that we are already enlightened, but that we have lost our way and need to get back to where we started. Since the Buddha's time, others have expanded on the concept of enlightenment. They see it not as what Andrew Cohen calls "a vertical lift-off, getting off the wheel of becoming, transcending this world absolutely, and leaving no trace," but as an evolution of consciousness that allows you to become an enlightened being in physical form. Babaji, Buddha, Sri Aurobindo, and Jesus Christ, among others, were all great beings who either came to Earth perfectly realized entities or were awakened while incarnated in their lifetime. They are avatars who guide seekers toward liberation.

What these teachers have demonstrated with their lives is how a spiritual path can expand from the small form of self to the higher Self that connects with the luminous, eternal Oneness of Spirit or God.

We flounder with the idea that we really don't know what drives this whole scenario called life. The Great Mystery encircles our universe with a web in which life can exist. Anything that has been written or taught throughout time is only the opinion of someone seeking to give meaning to this mystery. So when looking for answers simply sit quietly and look within.

One morning, while out walking, I was thinking about what this web might look like. Invisible to most eyes, it is there, nonetheless. Resting beneath a stand of old pine trees, I sat gazing down at the years' worth of fallen pine needles, layered upon the forest floor. There in front of me was the web. Nature mimicking the macrocosm of universal energy in the fall of pine needles upon the ground. Life's web has a breadth and depth that far exceeds our imagination.

Everything we learn in life is toward the goal of liberation from our afflicted minds and ultimately enlightenment. Isolated and alone, we miss the connection that inextricably binds us one to the other. Imagine if you could see the intricate web that wraps the universe in spiraling waves of energy. With our modern technology, we have tapped into this invisible matrix and manifest this power through cell phones, radio, television, and computers. This same omnipotence lies within the human spirit, a force that fuels our physical form. We tap into this phenomenal potential through the practice of meditation.

Practice

Nature's spiritual power can heal, strengthen, and enlighten when tapped into through meditation. It can inspire us to cultivate a reverence for the spirituality of the natural world that surrounds our lives.

Take some time to drive or walk out into nature. Go to a park nearby, hike along a wilderness trail, or take a trip to the beach. Don't set yourself any goals or predetermined destinations, just allow yourself the freedom to walk slowly and give your full attention to what surrounds you. Feel the movement of wind on your skin and in the leaves of the trees. Open your ears to the sound of the birds and of nature breathing all around you. From time to time, stop and stand still for a moment, absorbing the power that emanates from Earth's living presence.

Find a place to sit comfortably, perhaps with your back against a tree, close your eyes, and focus on your breath. As the mind calms and your thoughts begin to slow, allow the space between thoughts to grow longer. It is in the pause between thoughts that meditation exists. Recite the Earth mantra with each inhale and exhale.

Earth Mantra

Breathing in, I am fed by Earth's energy.

Breathing out, I live in the bounty of this moment.

After your meditation, take some time to write about your experience in your journal. Note the emotions and sensations that arose from within you. Continue to sit with your eyes open, stay focused on the present, and absorb the beauty around you.

Meditation and Religion

"In God's house there is no particular religion or sect of faith. To Him, all are the same."

—Baba Muktananda

The new millennium has heralded a quest by individuals for a deeper spiritual life, while, at the same time, they jump from one religion to another in an attempt to find some deeper satisfaction. Author Lauren F. Winner calls this "spiritual dabbling." She notes that when seekers are confronted with the reality that spirituality is hard work, frequently they move on to something else. What they fail to appreciate is that spiritual development takes time, for many a long, long time. The goal of any spiritual practice is to transform you, through prayer, ritual, and a realization of God. Faced with this transformation many people choose to run.

For many years I thought of myself as a spiritual seeker. I studied a number of religions, trying to find the "right" one for me. I had just begun my practice of yoga when my mother invited me to accompany her on a pilgrimage to Medjagoria, Yugoslavia. Once there I was climbing a small mountain to the place where the Virgin Mary is said to have appeared. The path was steep and littered with sharp rocks. I was mentally whining about the difficult climbing terrain, despite the expensive sneakers I was wearing.

Bounding up the path I passed the stations of the cross without stopping (making sure I got in a bit of aerobic exercise) when, rounding a big boulder, I came upon a group of people blocking my way. I looked around to see how I could go around them, maybe bypass the trail and climb hand over hand up the side to the next level above. Now that would be a challenge, I thought to myself, but great fun. Then something caught my attention. These pilgrims were barefoot. Some had rolled up their jeans and were crawling up the path, leaving pieces of skin and blood on the razor sharp stones. One man carried a young boy who was too sick and crippled to walk by himself. They prayed the rosary, and the sound of their weeping mingled with each Hail Mary.

I was dumbstruck. I had no idea what to do. I immediately recognized myself as a spiritual imposter, skipping along, paying no attention to what was really going on. I looked at the station of the cross carved into the mountain and saw Jesus carrying his cross through the streets of Jerusalem, the crown of thorns digging deep into his brow. I had made the journey to this shrine hoping to find peace, but at that moment I realized I had become a spiritual drifter. It had never even dawned on me that I would have to suffer physical pain to experience a spiritual awakening. I prayed that these peoples' prayers would be answered before mine might even be considered.

I had been going along thinking that by exploring this religion or that one, I was really doing some deep spiritual work. The illusion came crashing down on me in that moment on the mountain. I had been searching for my spiritual home and didn't see that what I was looking for was already within me.

Truly humbled, I prayed for guidance. In my meditations I saw the excuses I made for not moving forward with my life. What called me was a spiritual practice that transcends the limitations of our human existence to achieve oneness with God. I wanted a practice that I could bring into my daily life and use to help to change the world. When I left the shrine, I had renewed my commitment to a single spiritual practice (I chose the eight-limb path of yoga) and have never looked back.

A River Runs Through It

The process of living is a journey that takes us in many directions during our lifetime—often with surprising results. This is also true of your spiritual practice, which can be compared to taking a boat across a deep, wide river. The boat represents your spiritual practice, which carries you across the challenging "river" currents, rapids, and pitfalls of self-ignorance. Swami Veda Bharati, spiritual leader of the Himalayan Institute, says that reaching the other side of the river means you have attained self-realization, you have awakened to your authentic Self, and you can now leave the boat behind on the shore. The form that your spiritual practice takes, whether as a specific practice such as yoga, meditation, or Christianity, is just a means to an end. At the moment of Self-realization you no longer need the boat or system that got you there and you continue the journey "without means," in the realization of your authentic Self.

The Connection to God

You may already believe in the existence of God or have experienced the presence of something greater than yourself in your meditations. The spiritual journey can include the path of devotion to a Divine Spirit to whom you direct your prayers and compassionate works of service. As you read more about the many spiritual practices, you will encounter what appear to be contradictions in the teachings, yet they all point you toward the same direction, as the following examples illustrate.

Yogis who have attained complete knowledge say that God created the world for Him in which to play, and He can be seen in every part of it. The world is not a solid substance, not the final reality; it is a form of the Self, a play of divine Consciousness, a symbol of joy. The founder of Siddha Yoga, Bhagawan Nityananda was a great spiritual teacher of India. I include his teachings because they embody the guidelines for a spiritual practice that many follow today though they may have filtered through other styles of practice.

For Bhagawan Nityananda, all religions were equal. He saw all sects, all ideologies, and all philosophies as equal. He used to say that each sect or doctrine or creed is a different path leading to the same goal. Many paths lead to the same destination. Similarly, through all these different spiritual practices one can attain the same divine state.

The core of Bhagwan Nityananda's teaching is "The heart is the hub of all sacred places; go there and roam." The basis of the practice of self-realization or Siddha Yoga is, "Honour your Self, Worship your Self, Meditate on your Self, God dwells within you as you." According to Bhagwan, meditation is the most important part of this philosophy.

On the other hand, the Buddha didn't claim to be divine. He taught that he merely points the way to nirvana, but it is up to each individual to practice in order to get there. The concept of a personal God does not fit into the Buddhist system of religion. Buddhism teaches that all manifestations in the universe are God.

Zen master Shunryu Suzuki describes his concept of God as follows: "If God after making the world puts Himself outside it, He is no longer God. If He separates Himself from the world or wants to separate Himself, He is not God. The world is not the world when it is separated from God. God must be in the world and the world in God."

No matter how they differ in other aspects of their teachings, all these spiritual practices start from the belief that God is all pervasive and is part of all there is in the world. Which, naturally, includes us.

Prayer and Meditation

What is the best form of communication to use when communing with this Divine Spiritual power? In Christian meditation prayer is the foundation of the practice, whereas in other meditation disciplines the point is to do nothing. In these practices prayer and meditation are not the same thing. Meditation, practiced in the Buddhist tradition, teaches you to quiet the mind. In the Christian form of meditation, the mind is active, using prayer to connect to God or Jesus Christ. They both serve to focus your mind and teach you concentration, whereby you will eventually gain a deeper connection to Self.

Prayer is seen as a powerful medium in which to enact miracles. Scientist, philosopher, and spiritual teacher, Emmet Fox, writes that you can change a situation through the power of prayer. Regardless of the circumstances or what might have happened otherwise, enough prayer will get you out of your difficulty if only you will be persistent enough in your appeal to God. Jesus Christ devoted the greatest part of his ministry to the teaching of prayer. The miracles performed by Jesus came about because of his understanding of how prayer can work in one's life. This understanding, coupled with the Divine connection to his true Self, showed Jesus to be the epitome of human spiritual potential. He taught that "the works that I do, ye shall do, and greater works."

Mindful meditation is the act of mind-emptying as opposed to being mind-filling. It is not a form of prayer, nor is it a religion. It is, as psychotherapist David Richo explains, an exploration of how the mind works and how it can be stilled so as to reveal an inner spaciousness in which wisdom and compassion arise with ease.

Practice

There are times when I will begin or end my meditation practice with a prayer. I find that it gives me an immediate spiritual connection to the presence of Divine Spirit and helps me to focus and calm my mind. As I explained in Chapter 1, you can use a particular word or *mantra* to keep you present, but there may be moments when you will be agitated and unable to calm your mind. Perhaps not surprisingly, praying for peace—for yourself and for all beings—will bring some calm.

Sit in meditation and repeat the following Prayer mantra over and over again until your mind has calmed. Then focus on the inhale and exhale of your breath. When your mind begins to wander, come back to the Prayer mantra and repeat it again.

Prayer Mantra

Breathing in, I ask for peace amid this storm of emotions.

Breathing out, I pray that all beings may have peace in their lives.

When we pray for others we acknowledge that we are not alone amid our turmoil and confusion. By seeing our problems not as individual problems but as human problems, we will be better equipped to deal with them. Think of it like trying to swim out past high waves crashing onto the shore. Instead of walking straight into the force (in other words, facing your particular problems head-on) and being knocked off your feet, you wait for the perfect moment to dive into the center of the wave and swim beneath its power. Using prayer to get past your thoughts can work in this way.

Opening Our Connection to the Earth

"The Human Being within the Universe is a sounding board within a musical instrument."

—The Universe Story

When you are awakened in meditation, you become aware that you are connected to all that exists in the universe. And you're not just connected to other people, or even other animals and plants. You are part of every object—animate and inanimate—in the universe. When you begin to realize this, it's easier to understand how the nature of existence is just "to be" present to the flow and change that surrounds us.

Once when Bhagwah Nityananda was walking with his student Muktananda, along the bank of a river, they came to a huge rock near the path. "Do you see this rock?" the Swami asked Muktananda. "See the miracle? See the doing of the universal Consciousness? Here it has become a rock, here it has become a human being, and here it has become a tree. But although it has become all this, it does not lack Consciousness in its fullness."

Our early ancestors celebrated their lives within the embrace of nature and were aware of the tenuous line between the world of form and the world of spirit. They listened to the rhythms of the earth, the wind in the trees, the sounds of a wildness we have lost in our domestication and development of nature into cities and suburbs. What is integral to our survival as a species, as a world, is this return to listening to, and thereby connecting with, the universe. We are quick to make a connection with our cell phones, but to hear the owl call out on a winter's night, to understand the scolding of a raven, or to recognize the inner voice echoing from deep within our core is to hear the truth of our existence on this earth. It requires risking all your attachments, opinions, and beliefs, to dive through the opening that meditation provides.

Creating a Deeper Spiritual Life

"Be gentle with yourself. Be kind to yourself. You may not be perfect, but you are all you've got to work with. The process of becoming who you will be begins first with the total acceptance of who you are."

—Bhante Henepola Gunaratana

At some point in your spiritual path you will ask the age old question: "Who am I?" It is a step we each take when moving deeper into our exploration of what it means to be human. When you meditate, you have no choice but to look within yourself and see the deep emptiness and void: the shadow of death waiting at the end of all your efforts.

Now this is where it can get a bit heavy and you'll want to put down the book and switch on the TV, but stay with me here. You see, we view life as a hole that needs to be filled with pleasure, pain, food, drugs, excitements, sex, work, distractions, distractions, and more distractions. Most of all we fill it with fear. For this is what drives us: our unknowing, our total ignorance of what follows this lifetime, our simple-minded uncertainty of the Great Mystery that lies beyond.

Knowing yourself is the first and most important aspect of reaching the true Self. You can be certain that upon your spiritual path, you will want to get up off the meditation cushion and run away when faced with your mental monsters; but stay the course, use your breath to carry you over the obstacles, watch the thoughts come up and dissolve bringing the next thought close on its heels. Think of the process as peeling an onion. Each layer you remove brings you deeper to the center of your being. Along the way there will be tears and the strong smell of your own fears; as you persist, however, you will find at the heart lies the jewel of conscious awareness.

When I first began to meditate I would constantly fall asleep. It wasn't that I was tired, I just didn't want to face my thoughts and see myself with such blinding clarity. So for many months I would just practice my yoga postures, working to keep my focus centered on my breathing. Then I began to add a short meditation at the end of my practice, increasing the time slowly over many days until I was sitting for longer periods of time.

As you come to know yourself on the spiritual path, you will see how you are driven from your sense of lack, of not being good enough, of feeling empty and lonely. Rather than accepting your true Self, you make great efforts to change. Meditation gives you the tools to live in this void, open to it fully, rather than constantly running away and finding material distractions or people who will help you to stifle this feeling of emptiness.

Meditation awakens you to the spiritual journey we have undertaken as human beings. Knowing your spiritual and human self requires acceptance. You must clearly observe and accept all your flaws and weaknesses, understanding that they are part of human nature. Selfish, greedy, fearful, and suspicious, we cover up our fears by blaming others and justifying our rigid opinions. Mindful awareness opens you to the truth of who you are, a spiritual being having a human experience. This same awareness moves you past the miasma of mental chatter that distracts you from your spiritual path and from knowing your true Self.

Practice

Some days you will just want to sit quietly and let the breath lead you into a quiet mind. Then there will be times you will want to go deeper into yourself. Remember, with the shift and change of each moment your feelings will follow the same course. When you take your place on the meditation cushion or chair ask yourself what it is you need today and let the question fade as you bring your focus to the inhale and exhale of your breath.

Let your breath awareness give you time to focus and calm your mind. Now, visualize yourself surrounded with a mist of white light. See it in your mind's eye all around and above you, soft and delicate in nature. This is the light of Divine protection, providing a safe place for you to let go and relax fully.

Place your hands over your heart and recite the Heart mantra as you allow your breath to rise and fall naturally and gently.

Heart Mantra

Breathing in, My heart is illuminated.

Breathing out, I am filled with Divine light.

This should give you a wonderful feeling of being wrapped in a co-coon of love and warmth. It is as if the winter's fire has died down, and as you repeat the mantra you are blowing on the embers to bring the flame back to life. In this way your heart's fire is awakened and you connect to the deeper love of your Divine Self.

A Clear Mind: Spiritual Concentration

"Your own mind is the cause of happiness, your own mind is the cause of suffering. To obtain happiness and pacify suffering, you have to work within your own mind."

—Lama Zopa Rinpoche

A young monk went to his teacher and asked if the brain was the same as the mind. The old monk told his student that if he believed that his mind resided in his brain then he must find it and bring it to him. Essentially he was instructing the young man to explore the nature of his mind through observation of thought and how it functions. Does your mind have shape, color, or form? Where does it reside and from what point do your thoughts arise? Do your thoughts have substance or, in dissolving, do they leave no trace? Coming to understand the nature of your mind trains you for a deeper concentration in your spiritual practice.

The path described by Ashtanga Yoga, the eight-limbed path, includes concentration (*dharana*) as the sixth limb and occurs only after you have been able to establish a single pointed focus on an object, word, or breath. After sitting in meditation for 15 to 30 minutes, you should begin to feel your body getting lighter and more relaxed. In the back of your mind, you may be semiconscious of your body and your surroundings or you may have no awareness of them whatsoever. You can concentrate on the OM mantra, or the even flow of your breath. It is not unusual to experience a feeling of great happiness while in this state of concentration.

This happiness is not the same as pleasure that arises from sensual delight. It is important that you know the difference between focus, concentration, and meditation. Although they are each employed to gain freedom from the mind's afflictions, they are separate lessons on the path.

Dharana (concentration) and *dhyana* (meditation) have the power to sharpen the intellect. A trained intellect can comprehend subtle, philosophical, and complex problems, whereas a disciplined intellect can carefully differentiate the happiness derived from concentration and that of sensual objects. Knowing the subtle difference will free the mind from its attachment to sensual pleasures and create a lasting joy that emanates from deep within your true Self.

As you improve your concentration, new channels will form in the brain, new thought currents will be generated, and new brain cells will form. You are transformed on a cellular level. This constitutes the creation of a new mind, new feelings, new sentiments, positive emotions, and joy that fills your heart as you awaken to each new day.

Practice

This meditation brings in the elements of nature to help you return to your natural Buddha-mind. Take a moment to sit alone in silence, draw the curtains or the blinds, and light a candle and place it in front of you. Gaze into the candle's fire. Allow your thoughts to merge with the flame.

Repeat the Concentration mantra to draw your attention away from your mind's chatter. Then bring the light of the flame into your heart, feeling the warmth spread throughout your body. Keep your concentration on the fire's glow, letting all thought dissolve in your complete presence of the moment.

Concentration Mantra

> *Breathing in,* I steady my gaze.
> *Breathing out,* I am absorbed by the flame.

Watching the flame with open eyes trains the mind to concentrate. Having a point of focus helps prevent you from getting lost in the endless chatter of thought. This gazing on a single point of light expands your ability to stay present, leading you closer to full meditation.

Why We Suffer

If happiness is what we all are looking for why do we cause ourselves so much suffering?

Understanding why we cause ourselves to suffer is the first step in learning to let go of our attachments. Pema Chodron in her book *The Places That Scare You* describes how we suffer due to three misunderstandings:

- **We expect that which is always changing to be predictable.** Even though we can see that life is constantly shifting, we continue to live our lives thinking that nothing will change. We demand a sense of security in our lives and so we attach to the illusion of permanence in an impermanent world.

- **We go about our lives thinking we are separate from everything with a fixed ego identity.** Life is all about me, myself, and I. Whether we are building ourselves up to be something special or knocking ourselves down with self-criticism, the center of our universe is the irrefutable ego-driven self.

- **We look for happiness in situations that cause suffering.** We take many actions that provide a temporary relief from our afflicted emotions, but then turn around and whack us upside the head.

Alcohol and drugs dull the reality of your life, but then shift you right back into an even greater pain. Shopaholics have the distraction of buying things to fill the emptiness, but then are faced with the bills.

Food, drink, drugs, adventure, sex, and entertainment can be a whole lot of fun, but in the end they cause pain and suffering. Buddhist teachings tell us that these distractions keep us from bypassing the controlling ego and finding our true Self. Nonetheless, they are as much a part of the path toward liberation as restraint, compassion, moral conduct, and kindness. Every step you take is your path—all the difficulties as well as those moments of happiness. Our petty tyrants and challenging situations are the lessons we meet on our spiritual journey, in order to learn compassion and loving kindness. When life becomes difficult, we have to do something to ease the discomfort.

We are constantly trying to stabilize ourselves on a ship that is being tossed around in a storm at sea. Rather than go with the flow, we try to make life predictable.

I remember seeing a cartoon that summed up for me how unpredictable life can be. It was a picture of the corner of a brick building. Coming from the right is a peanut vendor, with his tray of peanuts hanging from his neck as he calls out, "Peanuts for sale." To the left, pressed up against the side of the building, lying in wait, is an elephant.

You never know what is waiting around the corner, but you can be sure that it will be something you didn't expect or plan for.

Moving Meditation: Selfless Giving

It may be that you don't have time each day to sit and meditate. Maybe you were sitting every morning and then things interfered and days would go by before you could find the time again. If you cannot always get to the cushion, try practicing loving kindness in other areas of your life. If someone you know needs assistance, a ride to the doctor, their child picked up from school, food waiting for them when they come home from work, any service you might provide will be an act of kindness on your part. Expect nothing in return for your kindness; and if they ask to repay you, tell them to pass it on to someone in need.

Kindness Mantra

Breathing in, My heart opens and gives love freely.

Breathing out, I ask only to serve so all may find happiness.

There are times when in doing a kind act we feel pressured for time and begin to resent our compassionate giving. This is when repeating the Kindness mantra in your mind will help keep you present to the task and away from watching the clock.

Guided Meditation: Our Spiritual Connections

Along the spiritual path you will learn to be compassionate toward others. This comes with recognizing your interconnectedness to all there is, even though this can be very difficult at times.

Compassion requires more of us than supporting someone with loving kindness; it involves our willingness to feel the pain of another. Feeling another's pain can be a difficult and overwhelming experience when first tried. So it is best to have in mind someone who is close to you.

Sitting comfortably, bring your focus to your breath and visualize the suffering individual in your mind's eye. See their suffering and pain in the form of a black smoke. As you inhale their suffering into your heart, it is important that you do not identify with the pain or the illness, but with the underlying energy. Visualize the black smoke becoming a pure white as you exhale peace and happiness to the person.

You can also do this practice with the suffering of all the people in the world. If it is not too overwhelming, breathe in the black smoke of suffering of all those in the world who are in pain and transform it to a pure white smoke, breathing out love and compassion from your heart in hope that all may find peace.

Compassion Mantra

Breathing in, I take in the pain and suffering of (name here).

Breathing out, I send (name here) peace and a release from suffering.

This is a powerful practice for opening your heart to the suffering of others. For in accepting their pain, you come to see that you are able to show compassion and loving kindness.

Chapter 3

Freedom from Fear:
Happy, Joyous, and Free

"You live in illusion and the appearance of things.
There is a Reality. You are that Reality. When you
understand this, you will see that you are nothing.
And being nothing, you are everything. That is all."
—Kalu Rimpoche

Underlining all of human motivations is a gripping sense of
fear. How will I survive? Will there be enough money to pay
the bills? Will he or she love me enough? The constant chatter
of the mind's concern with the fear of loss or change guides
our actions in almost every facet of our lives. Most of us have
lived under the shadow of this emotion for so long we don't
even notice it is there, working against our determination to
be strong.

As you sit in meditation and watch the thoughts arise,
you'll begin to understand the extent to which you are owned
by your fears. This doesn't mean that meditation will immediately make you less afraid or that it will be an easy process to

let go of your terror. It will, however, give you the chance to look your fears in the eye, get to know them, and see how unnecessary it is to carry them around with you.

In *When Things Fall Apart,* Pema Chodron writes that "Fear is a universal experience. Even the smallest insect feels it. It's not a terrible thing that we feel fear when faced with the unknown. It is part of being alive, something we all share. We react against the possibility of loneliness, of death, of not having anything to hold on to. Fear is a natural reaction to moving closer to the truth."

Owning Your Fears

"Fear is the mind-killer. Fear is the little-death that brings total obliteration."

—Frank Herbert

Fear is a natural part of life. It is what drives us in our reactions to everyday existence. It can save us in moments of immediate danger and motivate us to stand firm in face of a threat. But it can also freeze us into passivity in the face of overwhelming harm. When confronted by our fears, the natural inclination is to take one of the following actions:

- Run away
- Attempt to control it
- Try to suppress it
- Resist it in any way possible

Instead of avoiding your fears, you need to take off your blinders and face them. You will still want to run, control, suppress, or resist them; after you have seen what the monsters look like, however, you just might discover that they aren't such a big deal. The important thing is to identify your fears. Then, using meditation, you can observe them and work to dissolve them.

The majority of people live in fear of the unknown future. This may be fear of future failure, success, commitment, disapproval, a person, or group of other people, or even fear of looking at ourselves and seeing who we really are. In actuality, it is not the unknown we fear, but losing what we know, what we have, what we are attached to in our lives. Spiritual teacher J. Krishnamurti says that "you are afraid of discovering what you are, afraid of being at a loss, afraid of the pain which might come into being when you have lost or have not gained or have no more pleasure."

These fears limit your ability to flow with the ever-changing world. These fears stand in the way of actualizing your true potential.

It's not easy to face your fears, especially when you have set up an elaborate network of denial, subterfuge, and escape that has kept you dancing around your mental monsters. To help face down your fears, in your journal make a list of things you are afraid of. It might look something like this:

- Debilitating illness
- Loss of a loved one
- Pain and disfigurement
- Nuclear war

You might find that in making this list the little fears refuse to surface—things such as locking your keys in the car, getting a speeding ticket, or being late for a meeting. More than likely, you have a list of minor worries hanging around the backroom of your consciousness, draining energy and feeding into the big ones we all dread might happen. A good example of this is taking a minor health problem—say, a sore throat—and letting your imagination feed into your fear of having something more serious, such as throat cancer. Rather than dwell on these negative thoughts, use your meditation practice to calm your mind and emotions, so that you can see how you are just making up stories that have nothing to do with the truth.

Write Your Worries Away

In your meditation journal make a list of the minor worries that your imagination can grow into bigger concerns. They may look something like this:

- Being late to pick up your child from school and worrying that they might decide to walk home.
- Being late to work and missing an important meeting.
- Not having your work done on time and holding up your co-workers.

Now take each worry and carry it out to the worst scenario you can imagine, which is what the mind tends to do anyway. Notice that you are projecting into a future that does not exist and yet you have written, directed, and filmed the movie in your mind. Come back to the moment where none of your fears have taken place and sit quietly. Take the time to examine each worry and allow them to dissolve in the light of your awareness.

Once you realize that many of your fears are simply the result of your mind dwelling on the past or forecasting the future, you will be able to free yourself from these fears. If you live entirely in the here and now, you will have no fears, for everything is as it should be. When you identify your fears in meditation you will often have a good laugh over the absurdity of seeing just what is running your life.

Practice

Let's take a look at your fears, evaluate them, and ponder them in the light of reality. If they are something you can change, we will look at how you can do so. If they are irrational, you can let them go. As for those fears about which you can do nothing, the Tibetans say it best: If there is something you can do about your fear, then do it; if there is nothing you can do, then relax and stop worrying. Life is too short to waste time fearing what is not going to hurt you.

Sitting in meditation, focus on your breath and calm your mind. Begin by asking yourself "What am I afraid of?" and watch what arises in your mind. Use your meditation journal to record your observations, and ask yourself the following questions about each thing you fear:

- Is this a reasonable fear to have?
- What can I do about this fear?
- Is there any way to reduce the risk or the consequences?

For instance, suppose you are concerned about your family's well-being should something happen to you. Now that you've identified the fear, ask yourself each of the preceding questions as it relates to this fear. I provided some sample answers to help you get the ideas flowing:

- Is this a reasonable fear to have? *Yes, because I care about my loved ones.*

- What can I do about this fear? *I can take steps to protect my family should anything happen to me. I can also work to improve my health by eating better, getting enough exercise, and avoiding unnecessary dangers.*

- Is there any way to reduce the risk or the consequences? *I can take out a life insurance policy. That way, if I do die, I know my family will have enough money to live on.*

Here are some other possible fears and sample actions you can take to avoid them. You'll probably think of others—this is just to get your mind working in the right direction:

- Worried about old age? *Save more for retirement.*
- Afraid of skin cancer? *Cover up in the sun.*
- Afraid of sexually transmitted disease? *Practice safe sex or abstinence.*
- Afraid of environmental destruction? *Work for social change.*
- Afraid of getting fat? *Eat less and exercise.*
- Afraid of failing your exams? *Hit the books.*

Now begin to form a clear idea of what you will do to alleviate your fears and write down the appropriate action needed to do so.

If you find that some of your fears don't have an immediate solution, write about those fears in your journal and then come back to them the next time you meditate. For instance, suppose you are terrified by the possibility of a terrorist attack but aren't sure what to do about it. As you sit breathing quietly, you see that all that is taking place is you sitting and breathing. Now let the fear arise in your mind and see how it is drawn from TV images, newspaper stories, and your imagination. Just observe yourself quietly, without making any judgments about what you are seeing.

Let the old thoughts dissolve and create in their place thoughts of what you would like to see happen in the world. Replace your mental image of catastrophe with an image that reassures you and perhaps helps to create the conditions you do want.

Recite the Fear mantra with each inhale and exhale, allowing it to shift the tension and stress from your body.

Fear Mantra

Breathing in, I face my fears.

Breathing out, They dissolve in the light of love.

May all beings know peace and joy in their lifetime.

Visualize a white light emanating out from you, beginning in your solar plexus and slowly spreading throughout your entire body, bringing warmth and a feeling of peace. Now send this light out into the world, taking your fear and dissolving it with each exhalation of your breath.

Identifying the Mental Afflictions

"The mental afflictions are, by nature, relative and subjective; they have no absolute or objective basis."

—The Dalai Lama

At the root of all our mental afflictions is the fear of losing something we are attached to having—this is the cause of suffering.

The Buddha taught that all beings, without exception, are endowed with "buddhanature"—the heart of enlightenment—and that everyone has the potential to fully awaken to his or her truest state. This state is already present in our being, but it is awaiting discovery. In the practice of meditation, we aspire to connect with the inherent nature of goodness, openness, and purity in all beings.

Although the buddhanature is the natural state of our mind, we nevertheless experience various forms of confusion, disturbing emotions, and uncertainty. We fall under the influence of what in Buddhist teachings are called the three *kleshas,* or root mental afflictions:

- **Greed.** Grasping, attachment, clinging, fear of losing.
- **Hatred.** Ill will, aggression, aversion, fear of being opposed.
- **Delusion.** Illusion, ignorance, lack of awareness, fear of seeing the truth.

These mental afflictions block the perception of our true nature and are the cause for all actions that are harmful to ourselves and others. Notice how they feed into the fear of loss.

The offspring of these root afflictions are your old friends fear, jealousy, anger, and avarice. Each one feeds off the other as one thought builds into the next and then the next thought. Jealousy is the combination of fear, anger, and hurt: You are afraid of losing what you are attached to, angry because it is threatened with being taken away, and hurt from mentally projecting an outcome of pain. It doesn't matter if any of what you are agonizing about is based in truth; when you are in the throes of jealousy, you are trapped by your afflictions.

A student wrote to me about her insights into a relationship she has with a friend. She had been puzzled about the other's indifference to her and, upon waking one morning, saw the reality of the situation. She wrote that she had realized how much alike they were and that's why it was so painful for them to be together. She said, "We know each other's secrets, we love and hate each other, because we love and hate ourselves. We won't let anybody love us because we don't think we deserve to be loved. We are both fearful of letting the other get too close, because we think the other will find as much fault as we do in ourselves and will leave us anyway. We only truly feel safe alone."

She had seen the fear that blocked her connection to her friend, this same fear that keeps humans separate from each other—the fear of judgment, abandonment, rejection, betrayal, and loss of love. We are a bag of walking contradictions. We want to care more and then not care so much, we want to be honest and don't want to find out that our honesty is not enough. We justify our actions in fear of being misunderstood. We dance like a marionette to the mental puppet master in our heads.

As long as your mind is ruled or controlled by the thoughts that pass through it, you will suffer from fear and the root mental afflictions. It is only after coming to understand your true nature that you will be free of fear. However, you will need control of your mind in order to release the hold of your mental afflictions.

With the practice of meditation, you will achieve the state referred to as *emptiness*. When you recognize this nature and rest in it, all the mental afflictions that arise will dissolve into this emptiness, and thus be afflictions no longer.

Compassion and Loving Kindness

"In joy and sorrow all are equal, thus be guardian of all, as of yourself."

—Shantideva

Whenever I am stuck in a moment of anger, jealousy, or greed, I ask myself, "What's it all about, Quigley?" and immediately I am reminded that it is my commitment to become a more compassionate and loving human being.

Yes, well, easier said than done. Taking my practice of meditation out in the world gave me the opportunity to cultivate my spiritual practice by engendering love in place of anger and intolerance. When we are stuck in our negative thoughts and judgments about another person, we are only harming ourselves. The dark emotions feed our body with stress and tension, and literally can create an acid condition in the blood. The next time you are upset with someone, notice what happens to your mind and body, and then notice how the person you are upset with is just going about his or her life, probably not even aware of the damage you are causing yourself because of your attachment to him or her.

Swami Veda Bharati has an interesting way of expressing this teaching. Your anger is seldom about the object present. Let's say you are angry with someone in your life. The truth is, the anger is not about that immediate person or the situation. The anger just is. That's all. For you there is a mental conflict, perhaps something you haven't resolved from your past. These unresolved emotions or unsatisfied cravings or desires continue to run your life. And whenever an opportunity arises, they jump out and hook the object of your anger. In this way, you are dependent on the person you are angry with. Anger is the worst dependence, just as aversion is the worst attachment. Things you're averse to, persons you're antagonistic toward, that's what you are thinking of all the time.

Instead of thinking of people you love, you are thinking of the people who make you angry and irritate you.

How can something as simple as sitting and doing nothing—meditating—lead us toward becoming more compassionate?

It gives us a space in which to see ourselves and address our pain. In doing so we can better see others' pain and open our heart to what they are feeling. The Buddhist warrior practice of *Tonglon* means to exchange yourself for another. As you breathe in the pain and suffering of others, you send out love and happiness to the world. In Tonglon, you take on, through compassion, all the various mental and physical sufferings of all beings: their fear, frustration, pain, anger, guilt, bitterness, doubt, and rage. In exchange, you give them, through love, all your happiness, well-being, peace of mind, healing, and fulfillment.

Buddhist meditation teaches that the purpose to this lifetime is self-realization, which requires that you first clear away the illusion that shrouds your mind in order to perceive the reality of existence.

Amaro Bhikku, renowned spiritual teacher and Buddhist monk, says that, "Patient endurance is to hold steady in the midst of difficulty, to truly apprehend and digest the experience of dukkha, to understand its causes and let them go." *Dukkha* translates as suffering, unsatisfactoriness—the inherent insecurity, instability, and imperfection of conditioned phenomena. Combine a limited space with a certain ratio of bodies—a family (all with their opinions, experiences, and beliefs, vying for attention and demanding love)—and you have a challenge that requires awareness and a certain amount of respect.

Bliss Is Closer Than You Think

In the sacred scriptures of the Bhagavad Gita, God in the form of Krishna speaks to the warrior Arjuna and tells him, "He who controls his mind and has cut off desire and anger realizes the Self; he knows that God's bliss is nearer than near. Closing his eyes, his vision focused between the eyebrows, making the in-breath and the out-breath equal as they pass through his nostrils, he controls his senses and his mind, intent upon liberation; when desire, fear, and anger have left him, that man is forever free."

Freeing the Mind of Fear

"It takes courage to sit with pain, without avoiding or masking it; just to sit and face it totally and overcome one's fear."
—Joseph Goldstein

I am afraid. It starts when I hear the sound of gunfire in the woods surrounding my house. My state has just lifted a ban on shooting black bears, and I fear the sound signals the death of a bear. Because of suburban development pushing into the wilderness, bears have been coming face to face with their new neighbors, and tolerance is low. Rather than dealing with the perceived problem in a less violent way, authorities have decided to make it legal to shoot the wild creatures.

A large black bear makes her way through my yard each spring looking for food in the compost bin, and does so again during the summer months and then right before the hard winter snows fall. I consider her a part of my life and look forward to the visits. I respect her wildness and so do not attempt to approach or feed her, but I watch from behind my door the incredible spirit of this magnificent creature.

When I first heard the bear hunt was to progress, I was outraged and also afraid that the bear who pays me visits would be killed. Whenever I passed hunters on the road or heard the sounds of guns in the distance, my anger grew and my body ached with tension. I filled my mind with such strong judgments and negative thoughts that I was surprised at their intensity. Then one morning while I was meditating, I saw my emotional turmoil as an opportunity to move beyond my fears and judgment to a place of understanding and loving kindness. So I set about opening my heart.

First of all, I saw how fear was running the whole show—my fear for the well-being of my local bear as well as for all black bears, the hunters' fear of the bear causing harm to them or their loved ones, and the bears' fear. I had written letters of protest to the Governor, presented the issue on my radio show to encourage others to take a stand against the hunt, and now watched as our objections were ignored. In my meditation I was able to see both sides of the situation, but it did not dissolve the fear and anger. I continued to hold on to what I saw as an injustice, but one that goes deeper than being corrected with a simple solution. The needs of a growing population of human beings was intruding on the territory of the black bear and one had to step aside for the other. The reality was that I could not control development, but I can continue to educate others as to what we are doing to nature and all her creatures.

In my meditation I saw how I could transform my fear and anger to service. As I learn more about the issue I can share with others our connection to all that lives in our community and how to preserve the beauty and wonder of the natural world.

Is Your Foot on Fire?

Humans can be astonishingly fickle. We might feel for the suffering of a cat because we like cats, but not for dogs. We may send money to feed hungry children in Africa yet ignore a homeless person in our own neighborhood. We might be appalled at the conditions of caged chickens in factory farms and dine on grilled chicken breast for dinner. If we are to learn to be more loving and compassionate, we must practice with a consistency that extends itself to all beings. A Confucian saying compares the lack of humaneness to numbness and paralysis: To not feel compassion for a stranger in trouble is like not feeling that your foot is on fire.

Fear is what causes us to go to war against another country, pick a fight with another individual, or destroy a wild animal. Our fear of nature's unpredictability has us trying to control the weather, how our food is grown, the flow of rivers, and the growth of forests, to name just a few. Fear closes us down to alternative—less violent—responses and locks us into a mindset of intolerance and aggression. We hold on to our thoughts of being right rather than seeing our interconnectedness. We are the people we go to war against, and they are us. We intrude on the bears' territory and fear their reprisal.

Each time your fears arise, remember that they are mental states. You choose to hold on to them rather than let them dissolve.

Practice

You've listed your fears in your journal. Now go a bit further with this meditation. Read through the entire practice before beginning, to make sure that this is something you want to do. If you don't feel safe practicing this meditation on your own, but you want to continue, consider asking a trusted friend to read the instructions to you as you relax.

Begin by sitting comfortably. Imagine that you are surrounded by a protective white light. Within this light is only love and compassion. Within this protection, allow yourself to relax.

Now turn your awareness to your breath. With each inhale and exhale, feel yourself become calm as you watch your thoughts rise and fall away. Let each out-breath complete its task of freeing the air in your lungs. Let each in-breath arise naturally with no hurry. Let the process of breathing nourish your heart. Take your time.

Stay present to the moment. If you begin to wander, let go of the thoughts and let your breathing become the focus of your mind. When you are relaxed and feeling safe, think about something in your life that causes you to experience fear. Give this fear a name. What is this thing you are afraid of. Is it real or is it imaginary?

Remember that you are safe now. You are in a safe place, and right now this fear is only an object of your mind.

Notice the sensations in your body and the mental images that come with your fear. Allow them to come and go. Do not grasp and hold them, but notice them, appreciate them as warnings that something is out of balance. If the emotion becomes too strong, return your awareness to your breath and let go of the thought and the feeling. Surround yourself with the light of love and know that all is well at this moment.

If you are ready to face this fear, continue to breathe, continue to relax, but look squarely at the fear.

Feel your own power in the face of this object of aversion. Know that you have power. You have an inner strength to withstand or defeat the aversion. Feel the sensations that come with these thoughts.

Know that the emotions you feel come only from a thought. You can name the thought. You can change the thought. You can transform the image of fear in your mind into something different. Perhaps something funny. Perhaps something beautiful.

Recite the Freeing mantra to help you feel safe and present to the practice.

Freeing Mantra

Breathing in, I see my illusions.

Breathing out, I am safe and can let go.

Ask yourself: Is there any way this fear could be helpful to me? Notice what arises.

Ask yourself: What would have to happen for me to go beyond this fear? Let the answer show itself without judgment or denial, as if you were watching clouds passing overhead and then fading away.

Fear of Death

"Of all the world's wonders, which is the most wonderful? That no man, though he sees all others dying around him, believes that he himself will die."

—Bhagavad Gita

When I ask my friends or students what they fear about death, they usually tell me it's the unknown—not knowing what lies on the other side of living. For it is in that realm of sleep that we dream no more, and what is existence without our dreams and illusions? Some people fear getting up in the morning because they don't know what the day will bring. Others are afraid to love in fear of rejection, to sing in fear of ridicule, to dance in fear of being called foolish. Life is about dying each day and being reborn in the morning. Meditation is about dying to your old ways and uncovering your God Self.

Consider that it is not the unknown that you fear about death, but rather what you know about it, or at least what *think* you know about it.

In *The Experience of Insight,* Joseph Goldstein writes, "When we keep death at our fingertips we become less involved, less compulsive about the satisfaction or gratification of various desires in the moment." It is not a matter of dwelling on when we will die, but rather an acceptance that death is an inevitable ending to life so each moment is precious. With this way of seeing we are more inclined to let go of our attachments and stay open to love and generosity. Maintaining an awareness of our death, we can better experience the impermanence of all phenomena from moment to moment. Denying death keeps us in a state of fear and illusion.

The spiritual guru Osho taught that the moment you were born, you died. What he meant was that with birth, death has become a sure thing.

You are already dead, half-dead, because once you are born, you have come into the realm of death, entered into it. Now nothing can change it. Life and death are just like your two feet, your two legs. Life and death are both one process. Osha put it this way: Whenever you inhale, it is life, and whenever you exhale, it is death.

Practice

Here is a meditation practice, based on the teachings of Osho, that helps you to connect and relax your fear of death.

Sit comfortably with your eyes closed, exhale deeply, and while exhaling close your eyes.

When you exhale, space is created within, because breath is life. When you exhale deeply, you are vacant, life has gone out. In a way you are dead, if only for a moment. Enter into that silence of death. Air is moving out; you close your eyes and move within. The space is there, and you can move easily. The fear of death is not there, because now death appears like relaxation, death appears like a deep rest. Stay with the practice, building over time, until you can sit in this way for 15 minutes. At the end, recite the Peace mantra and you sit and breathe naturally.

Peace Mantra

> *Breathing in,* I relax.
> *Breathing out,* I am at peace.

Watch how this practice brings you a deep sense of peace and release.

Healing from Grief and Loss

> "If you do not bring forward what is within you, what is within you will destroy you. But if you bring forward what is within you, what is within you will heal and save you."
> —The Gospel of Thomas

We want the security of knowing that life will hold the pattern we create, the niche we carve out for ourselves in whatever space we can claim as our own. When we lose what we love, our pattern is changed forever, and we descend into grief. This time of grieving invites us to be still, to sit quietly and allow the process to unfold. We might think that some kind of action needs to take place, some moving on from the sadness; in fact, it is in giving time to your grief that it becomes a transformative experience.

When a close friend died of cancer, many people in my circle of friends were devastated by the loss. I remember waking up the morning after he died knowing that the world had changed forever, and I right along with it. I found myself looking at each moment as if he would appear again in my field of vision. I felt so weighed down with sorrow that there was nothing to do but sit in emptiness.

Even knowing his illness was terminal, those of us around him refused to acknowledge that he was dying. Later, when we looked at pictures, taken days before his passing, we were shocked at what was so evident. The man was dying, and we couldn't let him go.

When we lose someone or something we love, we are faced with the space that person held and we fill it with grief and longing.

Grieving is the emotional healing our mind needs to recover from loss. If we are unable to grieve our losses, we have difficulty moving on. We forfeit some of our emotional flexibility. Our psyches develop hard spots, which may manifest themselves in habitual anger, irritability, anxiety, depression, or addiction.

Taking my grief to the meditation cushion, I sat and watched my breath, cried, sobbed, blew my nose, and watched my breath some more. There were mornings I couldn't sit still and was overcome by sadness again, and so I would do my yoga, moving from one posture to another. Gradually, what I called the "grief balloon" began to deflate, and this incredible feeling of love was there to fill the space. My attachment to my friend's death had dissolved, and I was filled with the purity of unconditional love that had formed the basis of our relationship.

Joseph Goldstein writes that love that comes from wisdom is an "unconditional, universal loving kindness—a feeling of friendliness and warmth for all beings everywhere." All that you can do to shed your grief and replace it with love is to be patient, do the practice, and meditate. That's all that's required.

Practice

So often in our culture we are told not to show our emotions, and so grief gets locked away deep inside. You imagine that it is gone; unless you have worked it out, however, it is there, gnawing away on your psyche and body. In this meditation, take a moment to sit comfortably. Have your journal nearby to note any insights.

Bring your focus to your breath and allow your mind to calm as you watch any thoughts arise and pass away. Begin to look back over your life. Begin with your childhood and bring to mind an experience in which you might have had of loss. Perhaps it was a favorite pet, a friend, or a parent. If it becomes too painful, focus on your breath or stop and write what you are experiencing in your journal. Look over the following questions and observe what comes up in your mind:

- How did I respond to the loss at the time?
- What do I think and feel about it now?
- How much of the pain is still with me?
- Did I allow healing to occur, or is the wound still open?
- Can I allow healing now?
- Is there any reason that I might be preventing healing from happening?
- Do I blame myself or someone else for my loss?
- Can I now forgive them?
- Can I accept that the loss happened—that right or wrong this is the way things are?
- Can I acknowledge the depth of the loss?
- Can I honor the loss, and honor my grief, while carrying on with life?

Remain seated and keep watching your breath. Know that you are safe. If you start to cry, don't try to stop it. Crying is your body's natural way of releasing what is bottled up inside. Say the Forgiveness mantra to yourself, with each inhale and exhale.

Forgiveness Mantra

Breathing in, I forgive.

Breathing out, I am filled with love.

Oftentimes with the loss of someone we love, it may be we need to forgive that person or be forgiven for any misunderstandings. On the inhale, breathing in, "I forgive" can be changed to "I am forgiven." Know that the Universe and God sees you as already perfect, embodying the seed of loving compassion. This is not something you must earn, but qualities that are already a part of your human nature. That's why the practice of meditation is so important—it reveals the depths of love that you are capable of living.

Moving Meditation: Facing Your Fears

What is it that *you* are really afraid to do (whereas most other people do the same thing with ease and confidence)? In your meditation journal make a list of things that you are afraid to do, such as ...

- Stand up in front of a group of people and sing.
- Do a headstand.
- Swim across the swimming pool.

This practice is an opportunity to look at what your fears are made of and take the steps to overcome them. This may involve taking a few singing, yoga, or swimming lessons. With the guidance of a knowledgeable teacher, you can learn to overcome your fears by first learning how to control the situation.

Sit in meditation and consider your list of fears. Pick one to start with. If it is getting up to speak in front of a group, then imagine yourself doing this and notice the fear that arises. Now observe what is behind the fear. If it is a memory, allow it to arise so that you can see how you are held by something that happened in the past, but is irrelevant in the present. Recite the Fear mantra to help dissolve this limitation.

Fear Mantra

> *Breathing in,* I am whole and complete.
>
> *Breathing out,* Life supports me in all that I do.

Take the steps to find a teacher or workshop where you can safely learn to speak in public, to dance, to sing ... you get the idea. But most of all enjoy the freedom in letting go of your fear.

Guided Meditation: Releasing Your Fear of Love

The fear of loving or being loved can stem from old hurts and disappointments from the past. This kind of fear only holds you back from experiencing your true loving nature. Here is a meditation practice that will help take you through the process of dissolving your fear of loving and opening your heart to give and receive love.

Sit in a comfortable position, with your eyes closed, and take a few deep breaths. Now breathe naturally, allowing the mind to calm and focus.

In your mind, visualize a cloud of white light surrounding you. Breathe in, and take this healing energy into your lungs, your cells, and your heart. Bring your focus to your heart and allow the white light to cleanse any negativity that may have caused you to feel pain.

With each breath, let your fears about love arise, and watch as they dissolve as they are seen in the light. Be willing to release your fear of feeling love. Continue to stay present. Do nothing else except breathe. Keep the intention to heal yourself of the fear of love.

Now allow the light to cleanse you of any fears you may have about giving love. With a deep breath, be willing to release the fear that if you give love you could be controlled, abused, deceived, betrayed, maimed, or hurt in any way. Allow all of these fears to be lifted completely, and feel your heart expanding to its natural loving state.

Say the Love mantra to yourself with the rise and fall of each breath.

Love Mantra

Breathing in, I dissolve my fears in the light.

Breathing out, I open my heart to love fully.

Releasing your fear to love or receive love opens you to experience the ultimate goal of buddhanature. This is the love that permeates the universe. It is the foundation at the core of our being, resting as a jewel in the palm of God's hand.

Chapter 4

True Blessings:
Patience and Tolerance

"Act as if the future of the universe depends on what
you do, while laughing at yourself for thinking that
your actions make any difference."
—Buddhist saying

How many times have you said, "I wish she would hurry
up!" or, "I can't stand him!"? Often, I suspect. Our society
encourages impatience and intolerance of the faults of others.
How do you learn patience in a world that is racing past so
fast you can barely keep up?

Through film, television, radio, and the Internet, we are fed
a stream of information and images that constantly bombard
our senses with stimulus. Information is distributed in "sound
bites," while the advertising media demands that you have it
all now, today, 10 minutes ago. We want fast food and instant
gratification. If we don't get the parking space we raced
across the lot to nab, we erupt in anger. We are taught from
infancy that to be impatient is how one deals in our culture.

To counter these negative energies, we sedate ourselves with food, alcohol, mind-numbing TV, and drugs, hoping to find some calm amid the storm. In the end, we are only feeding into the frenzy and harming ourselves in the process.

The Buddha's teachings of the Four Noble Truths (see Chapter 1) tell us that if we are to gain freedom from suffering, we need to understand the causes and conditions that gave rise to suffering and strive to eliminate them. We must also understand what causes and conditions contribute to our attainment of happiness and actually practice them. One of the great lessons we receive when we face ourselves on the meditation cushion is learning to be patient and tolerant with ourselves.

Meditation teaches you how to slow down your world and bring calm to your agitated mind. It can help you to find respite from the constant onslaught of the surrounding world. As it teaches you to slow your thoughts, to be fully awake in the moment, the race to go nowhere fast falls away, leaving you with a great peace and well-being.

Learning Patience and Tolerance

One afternoon I was standing in line at the supermarket. I was in a hurry to get the shopping done and the cashier was making small talk with the customer in front of me. She slowly bagged the groceries as the two of them caught up on each other's lives. I could feel my patience growing thin as my mind played critic to what I perceived as the cashier not doing her job properly. As I noticed myself shifting from one foot to the other in agitation I suddenly recognized a great opportunity to let go of what I wanted to have happen. So I shifted my perspective and saw the cashier as a hardworking individual who was making her time more pleasant by interacting with the customers in a positive way. Rather than do her job in a non-personal manner she chose to interact with the people she saw every week buying their groceries. I saw that she was living in the moment rather than merely enduring the hours until she could go home. Seeing this allowed me to relax and let go of my impatience. When it was my turn the cashier greeted me with a big smile and asked about my day.

Let Go of the Anger and Impatience

The next time you are in a situation that stretches your patience, making you tense and angry, take a few deep breaths and pay attention to what is happening in the moment. Shift your perspective to see if there is another way to look at what is taking place. Put yourself in the other person's shoes before making a final judgment. Think about how you are breathing and focus on releasing any tension with the exhale of your breath. Remember that any anger you are holding on to in this moment can have a negative influence on the next moment, and the next, and the next …

My student Christine's mother lay dying of throat cancer. She had come to be with her at the end and was extremely uncomfortable seeing her mother suffering. One evening she heard her mother in the bedroom speaking softly to herself. "I am afraid," she said. Christine came to her side and asked her what she was afraid of. "I'm afraid of dying," her mother replied.

In that moment, Christine was overcome with apprehension and concern for herself—she didn't want to lose her mother. Her mother needed her, but her feelings told her to get up and run. "I put aside my emotions and sat down to help my mother move toward her death, despite my feelings of discomfort. I had to shove down my need to make it all about me and instead make it all about her, about the way she wanted to die. I came to understand what constitutes tolerance in a whole new way."

The Path of Patience and Tolerance

Patience allows for the natural flow of events to unfold.

Impatience tries to rush things into happening.

Patience tolerates our differences with room for understanding.

Impatience sees only one side.

Tolerance allows us the space to do what we need in the moment.

Intolerance tries to control others' actions.

Tolerance accepts our differences.

Intolerance condemns what is different.

Patience gives us time to see that the job is done right.

Impatience hurries us into accepting mediocrity.

Patience is a form of unconditional love.
Impatience is about satisfying the ego.
Tolerance gives us the freedom of choice.
Intolerance denies our right to freedom.
Patience allows time for living in the moment.
Impatience lives in an undetermined future.
Tolerance allows for forgiveness to happen.
Intolerance judges and condemns.

An afflicted mind trapped in the separation of self from others—stimulated by sugar, caffeine, and drugs; and running to keep one step ahead of the monthly bills—is not the ideal breeding ground for finding tolerance and patience. Bringing calm and insight through meditation allows tolerance to arise from a state of mental relaxation. As we learn to train the mind, we are able to remain calm in situations in which we might once have lost patience. We can also begin to see how others act out their lack of emotional control and how we can stand as a support to their explosive nature.

Consider the big picture when confronted with a situation between two angry people. You can see how they are each holding on to the need to be right. There is no tolerance for each other, no patience with working out the details, no listening to what is being said and, consequently, no understanding.

I asked my yoga students how the practice of meditation and yoga had helped them to learn patience and tolerance. One woman, in her mid-50s, told me how she could never stay the course when difficulties would arise. When she wasn't happy with herself because she had a few extra pounds, or her balance was off during class, she would become so impatient and want to give it all up. Through her practice, she was able to accept her limitations, to look at the bigger picture—the spiritual picture—that would give her a focus, something deeper than her own personal limitations. In this way, she was able to love herself with patience and caring.

Looking at a bigger spiritual picture helps to broaden your vision, open your narrow field of focus to encompass the whole of life, an evolution of character, a letting go of ego. Looking at the big picture can bring more meaning to a situation you might normally rush through or shrug off. When you have been sitting in meditation for a period of time, you get to see how your thoughts lack substance, like cotton candy, pure fluff. You also see how a narrow range of focus is much like eating a plain bagel for breakfast, lunch, and dinner. The lack of variety limits the nutrients you need to feed your body and mind.

A beginning yoga student came to one of my more advanced classes, asking if she could take the class. I told her only if she paid strict attention to her abilities and was able to stay present to her body. While attempting a difficult posture the other students were doing easily, she began to push herself close to a dangerous edge. "I was trying to be like everyone else and I remember that you came to me and asked why I was in such a hurry to get there. There was no need to rush. There was nowhere to go, but just be in the moment. It was my lesson in learning to be patient with my body and tolerant of my limitations."

Practice

Find a moment when you can sit quietly in meditation. Bring your attention to the rise and fall of your breath and allow your thoughts to fade into the background. Remember a recent experience in which you became impatient. Perhaps you wanted your children, spouse, or colleague to act a certain way and, when they didn't, you lost your patience. Or maybe you were impatient with yourself as you attempted to accomplish something that required more time and thought than you had to give to it.

Let the memory arise so that you can observe yourself in the moment of losing your patience. Notice how your body felt, the state of your mind, the words you used to convey your frustration, the tension trapped in your body. This is not a time to judge or justify what took place, but a way to learn about yourself through observation. Allow the breath to dissolve the tension in your body until you are totally relaxed.

Ask yourself whether there was another way you could have handled the situation. Perhaps you might have made sure the chain of events leading up to the action had allowed you more time to get things done, or perhaps you might have looked at the other person's side of the story before jumping to conclusions and assuming he or she was wrong.

Explore what those possibilities might be and then let them all dissolve in the flow of your breath. Recite the Patience mantra, bringing calm and ease into your heart and lungs.

Patience Mantra

> *Breathing in,* I expand my patience.
>
> *Breathing out,* I stay present to the moment.

Being aware of what is happening in the present is important for cultivating patience. Running ahead, always imagining the future, leaves you no tolerance for what is going on around you. Use this practice to keep you grounded.

Turning Intolerance into True Kindness

How do you change your intolerant attitude toward others to feelings of compassion and loving kindness? Through meditation practice. All the people and things in your life that cause you suffering are challenges to help you learn compassion and loving kindness. The Dalai Lama says that the kindness we express must cover all sentient beings—in particular, our enemy. If you feel anger and cannot think about kindness toward the enemy, this attitude must change. To develop true kindness, you must have a strong tolerance. Without tolerance and patience, you cannot find the means to generate a sense of love.

Someone whom we oppose, the tyrant boss who demands you work overtime, the neighbor who is always complaining about something, the co-worker who is angry and ill-tempered, these individuals upset our lives and become the enemy for whom we have bitter feelings. These people give us the chance to develop tolerance and patience. A fierce enemy is our best teacher. We can use our enemy's ruthlessness to develop and hone our feelings of tolerance and patience. After we've learned to be tolerant of and patient with our enemies, we are on the path toward developing infinite kindness and altruism toward all beings, and we have begun to open our heart to the world.

Opening your heart can be a scary and uncomfortable thing to do. You may remember as a child the trust and innocence you felt with other people and how, over time, hurt and disappointment, jealousy, grief anger, and resentment caused you to close your heart from pain. Now just when you have it locked away in a safe place I ask you to open that secret place and bring your heart out into the light.

Meditation teacher Sally Kempton focuses on teaching what she calls, "the power of the heart" meditation. This is a specific meditation for releasing the strictures we place on our hearts and allows us to be open to accepting and giving loving kindness. Kempton says that the heart is who we are, in the true sense. When you come to stand in the heart, you can free yourself from the oppression of your fear, your pain, and confusion. In this space you will feel a connection with all beings in the universe. The essence of meditation is to explore the heart, to let it reveal its wisdom and love to us.

In our practice of meditation, we discover how to awaken our heart. When we return to the heart again and again, there will come a day when we find ourselves living in the heart, from the heart, and for the heart.

Practice

Sit comfortably and focus your attention on the area of your heart. Inhale deeply and visualize filling your heart with a deep green light. The color green represents love, kindness, compassion, and generosity. It is also the color of nature, the chlorophyll that runs through the veins of plants and ultimately feeds oxygen to our blood. As you exhale, see this green light surrounding someone you wish to send love and kindness to, or wrap the earth in this powerful healing energy. Continue to do this for five breaths.

Now bring your attention back to breathing normally, without forcing or trying to make anything happen. Notice the energy in your body and again focus on your heart.

This time as you inhale, see the deep green light coming into your heart, filling your whole being with this warm loving light. When you exhale, let it release slowly as you hold the green light deep within your heart. Repeat this for five breaths.

Throughout you can recite the Kindness mantra, which will help to keep you centered in the heart space.

Kindness Mantra

Breathing in, I accept the light of love.

Breathing out, I feed the whole world.

Colors are often related to emotions. The color green represents the heart chakra and stands for love, kindness, compassion, and generosity.

Living as an Example

"Life responds when we risk."

—Rodney Smith (*Lessons From the Dying*)

Wanting people to change will challenge your lessons on patience and tolerance. As you begin to experience many of the positive benefits of meditation, such as ...

- Feeling more relaxed.
- Having more patience.
- Becoming more aware and focused.
- Feeling less anxious.

You'll want to share your experience with the people around you so that they will feel as good as you do.

When sharing your insights about the transformative aspects of meditation with family and friends, it is difficult not to preach or lecture to them, telling them how they should "be." After all, you got it, so they should be able to as well, right? Most people don't like to be told what to do, they don't like to hear that "if you don't meditate you're lost" or be treated to Bible-thumping evangelism.

When my students tell me about how difficult it is to get their loved ones to meditate I tell them to do their practice and teach by example. This requires patience, since they want to share what is important in their lives with their mates and friends, but I have found that those around you will notice the positive changes by the way you live your life. Toward the end of his life the Buddha told his followers to be a light by which others may see. He meant that by your actions and your deeds you will lead others to transform their lives.

So how do you get your message across?

Simply by living with a pure mind (what the Buddhist's call *parami,* the yogis call the *Yamas* and *Niyamas,* and Christians call grace), you will attract those people who are ready to ask "what are you doing that gives you this calm and joy in your life?" Through the practice of meditation and the quality of your actions in daily living you can create a state of pure mind.

A scattered and distracted mind is careless and unable to see the results of its actions. It has no patience or tolerance for those it encounters from day to day. With meditation you cultivate insight awareness, which gives you a calm mind—one that's able to see that all is changing and impermanent. There is nothing to cling to or grasp at; and as you experience the flow of life in and around you, you can let go and surrender to the immediate moment.

With this insight awareness you can take the patience and tolerance you learn on the meditation cushion and practice it in every facet of your life, with your family, co-workers, friends, salespeople, and children. This is where you learn how to live in the world without getting attached to others' illusions of how life should be lived.

I have observed that there is a definite difference in how meditators and nonmeditators make decisions. Experienced meditators are so focused in the moment that they can discern what is immediate and take action without being encumbered by the past and future. Nonmeditators tend to hesitate, mentally dance around the issue, doubt their intuition, and become distracted by the incessant chatter of their thoughts. Experienced meditators are able to remain calm and patient in an emergency with an eye to what is needed in that moment rather than operating out of fear and panic.

For the meditator these qualities arise naturally without having to think about them. They have been cultivated through practice, right intention, and having trained the mind to live in the present moment. The best way to learn patience and tolerance comes from dealing with your small, ego-driven self, that part of your mind that controls the need to survive in the chaotic world around you and clouds your mind with irrelevant thoughts and emotions.

Taking Righteous Action

"Who will speak for the birds and the bees, the children and
those who cannot speak, if we do not?"

—Dr. Wally Burnstein

Taking your understanding of the wrong being done in your community, country, or the world and turning it to compassionate action is the
inevitable step on the path to freedom from intolerance and impatience.
As you awaken from seeing the world only as you wish to view it and
encounter the reality of suffering on every level of life, you will want to
be of service to those in need of kindness.

Dr. Wally Burnstein was a doctor who saw the wrong being done in
the world and stepped out of his comfortable life to try and make some
things right. One day he went to see the senator of his state to discuss a
particular food-contamination issue. The senator leaned back in his chair
and said, "Well, Dr. Burnstein, how can we compromise on this issue?"
Wally leaned across the senator's desk and said, "What kind of compromise are we talking about, senator? Your children develop cancer or
mine do?" To Dr. Burnstein the only compromise was for the senator to
help stop the threat to others' health and well-being.

The doctor's work as an activist required tremendous patience for the
slow grind of the political machinery as well as tolerance for those who
were blind to the environmental destruction going on around them. At
the same time he refused to tolerate the suffering inflicted on innocent
people by others seeking monetary gain. He once told me that he had
learned patience from the process of creating change, yet he constantly
wrestled with his impatience for the injustice and harm being caused in
the world.

When working to preserve and protect your community you will
experience the same frustrations that Wally Burnstein felt as he grappled
with the lessons of patience and tolerance as a peace and justice activist.
Combined with a daily meditation practice you will be able to see more
clearly what needs to be done and what actions need to be taken when
confronting important issues that require stepping out of your comfort
zone and into the world of confrontation.

The Song of Songs

I came upon *The Song of Songs* while reading the Kabbalah. It seems to describe the path one takes toward recognizing our enlightenment. It speaks of bringing our understanding, patience, tolerance, compassion, and loving kindness out into the world, moving from our communities, to our countries, to the world, and eventually to all of the universe.

There is one who sings the song of his soul, discovering in his soul everything—utter spiritual fulfillment.

There is one who sings the song of his people. Emerging from the private circle of his soul—not expansive enough, not yet tranquil—he strives for fierce heights, clinging to the entire community of Israel in tender love. Together with her he sings her song, feels her anguish, delights in her hopes. He conceives profound insights into her past and her future, deftly probing the inwardness of her spirit with the wisdom of love.

Then there is one whose soul expands until it extends beyond the border of Israel, singing the song of humanity. In the glory of the entire human race, in the glory of the human form, his spirit spreads, aspiring to the goal of humankind, envisioning its consummation. From this spring of life, he draws all his deepest reflections, his searching, striving, and vision.

Then there is one who expands even further until he unites with all of existence, with all creatures, with all worlds, singing a song with them all.

There is one who ascends with all these songs in unison—the song of the soul, the song of the nation, the song of humanity, the song of the cosmos—resounding together, blending in harmony, circulating the sap of life, the sound of holy joy.

As you walk the path that leads to enlightenment, take your courage and step out into the world to see with new eyes the reality of what society has created. Consider how you might help adults who are in abusive relationships or children who have no one to look out for them. When you stand for speaking the truth, how can you abide the lies told to communities that watch their children sicken from contaminated air and water generated from negligent factories and power plants? As you practice sexual moderation, can you continue to tolerate the abuse of women and children in exploitative pornography? The world is filled with wrongs that must be righted; and although you cannot be expected to take them all on, consider how you can be of help.

Practice

Look around your community or in your local newspaper for a situation that stands out to you. Make a list in your meditation journal of important changes that must be made. Look over the list and see how you can best support these causes.

Perhaps you have a few hours a week to volunteer in a soup kitchen or work on a telephone hotline. For others, you might commit a certain amount of your monthly income to help support the cause of an organization that speaks to your heart. Perhaps you're interested in helping women in third world countries receive an education so they can support their families. Or maybe you want to send money to an organization that gives cows and goats to poor families, so they can live from the milk and cheese the animals produce. With a few moments of your time, you can contribute needed resources to people who have no hope of receiving help were it not for you and others like you.

Generosity Mantra

Breathing in, I give freely to those in need.

Breathing out, I let go and surrender my grasping nature.

You might wonder what one person can do to effect change in the world. If each person practices patience, change will happen. If each person practices tolerance for the different ways that change can take place, the world will shift toward a higher state of consciousness as more love is poured into the river of humanity.

A Simple Story

Sometimes a simple parable can be a powerful lesson. Here is an old story, from *Jivamukti Yoga,* that illustrates the importance of patience and tolerance, and how an understanding of the impermanence of all things can be liberating.

There was once a farmer who lived with his wife, his son, and one horse. The family planned to enter the horse in the annual county fair and hoped it would win prizes that could lead to breeding opportunities. This would ensure a nice future income for the farmer and his family.

The night before the fair, a violent storm swept over the countryside. When the farmer and his family awoke early the next morning, they found that the fences had been blown down. Their prize stallion was nowhere to be found. The farmer's wife was beside herself with despair. The neighbors came and joined in the wife's grief. "What terrible misfortune has befallen us!" cried the wife. "Yes, yes, this is most unfortunate," the neighbors agreed. But the farmer said, "Fortunate or unfortunate, I don't know. Let's wait and see."

A week passed and the farmer and his family were sitting at the breakfast table. Looking out the kitchen window, they saw a herd of horses galloping toward the farm. It was their faithful stallion, leading five horses and a little filly behind him. He had found a herd of wild mares, and now he was bringing them home. The farmer's family ran out to open the corral gate for the horses. The farmer's wife was overjoyed and exclaimed, "What a fortunate turn of events, this is unbelievable!" The neighbors rushed over, exclaiming, "How fortunate you are!" The farmer just said, "Fortunate or unfortunate, I don't know, let's wait and see."

Over the next weeks, the farmer and his son were busy training the new horses. One day the son was thrown by one of the wild horses. He suffered a bad fall and broke many bones. The farmer's wife was very upset. Between her sobs, she said, "We never should have let those wild horses in; this is a most unfortunate accident. My poor son." The neighbors came to commiserate with the wife about her misfortune. And the farmer said, "Fortunate or unfortunate, I don't know. Let's wait and see."

Two days later, the king's soldiers came by the little farm. The king had declared war on an adjacent country, and the soldiers had orders to draft all able-bodied young men into the army. On seeing the farmer's son with both legs and both arms broken, they left him home and continued on to the next family. The farmer's wife wept with relief, crying, "How lucky we are! This is most fortunate." The neighbors, most of whom had had sons taken off to war, said, "You are indeed most fortunate." The farmer said, "Fortunate or unfortunate, I don't know, let's wait and see."

Some months passed and the farmer's son was recovering very nicely. One day a messenger arrived from the king's palace to see about the son's health. Seeing his improved condition, he stated by order of the king that the son must come at once to the palace to work in the gardens and stables. The wife was bitterly angry, cursed the king for his unfairness but let her son go. "How unfortunate we surely are!" she said. "We have lost our son, and there will be no one to help us with the farm now." The neighbors came by to console the wife, murmuring, "What an unfortunate turn of events." The farmer just said, "Fortunate or unfortunate, I don't know, let's wait and see."

Now the king had a beautiful daughter. One day she looked out of her window and saw the handsome new gardener. She fell in love with him and went to her father and said, "Father, I have found the man I wish to marry. The king loved his daughter and wanted her to be happy, so he promised to make it happen.

The next day a messenger was sent from the palace to the farm, bearing a wedding invitation for the farmer and his wife, as well as an invitation for them to come live permanently at the palace. The farmer's wife was overjoyed. "We are so very fortunate," she said. The neighbors exclaimed, "Indeed, this is a very fortunate turn of events!" And the farmer, as usual, said ....

You see the farmer saw the impermanence of life and remained detached from the ups and downs, the pleasure and pain, the cycle of attachment. He was able to stay free while those around him were not. He demonstrated how what you learn from your meditation practice can be lived on a daily basis, helping you to deal with whatever shows up in your life.

Moving Meditation: Observing Nature

Step outside into your yard or go out for a walk. Keep your awareness in the moment and look around you at the plants growing in your area. Notice how nature has patiently grown to tolerate the development that has sprung up over the years. You can see how a blade of grass has pushed up through concrete to reach the sunlight, how a dandelion has bypassed all efforts of eradication to take root and emerge into the light. Trees that survive along toxic highways stand tall and proud, giving off life-saving oxygen. Observing the patience of nature brings us into a meditative state of wonder.

Now return to your sacred space and sit in mediation. Remember the plants you have just seen and receive their determination to live fully, without lashing out at their surroundings but rather adapting to the situation at hand. Recite the flow mantra to help focus you in the moment.

Flow Mantra

Breathing in, I allow the moment to unfold in its own time.

Breathing out, I embrace the world.

Allow the flow of your breath to deepen your awareness of how long it has taken your life to unfold, one breath at a time, one step in front of the other. All life follows a pattern of birth, growth, death, and rebirth. In meditation we see how each piece must form and shape itself before manifesting in the here and now. In knowing the way life moves, we become a part of the evolution and find our proper place in the scheme of things.

Guided Meditation: Awakening Tolerance

Sit comfortably and bring your focus to your breath. Watch your thoughts arise and pass away without engaging them. Now bring your awareness to how you view other people of the world, people of different ethnic backgrounds, religions, or skin color. Notice what arises in your thoughts—any judgments, criticisms, feelings of indifference, or harsh emotions.

Notice where these feelings come from. Observe any fear that lies at the root of your intolerance and bring it forward into the light of your scrutiny.

Ask yourself the following questions:

What makes me so different from others that I can judge them?

What do I fear will happen from those I cannot tolerate?

How can I see them in a more compassionate light?

How can I understand their place in this world?

You can use your journal to write down any insights that appear for you or any emotions that arise. Use the Tolerance mantra to open your heart and express loving kindness for all those toward whom you have felt enmity.

Tolerance Mantra

Breathing in, May my heart open with compassion for all beings.

Breathing out, May all beings cease to suffer.

Breathing in, May all beings find peace and happiness in their lifetime.

Open your heart and send your love out into the world. As each of us transforms our lives and finds the heart of our true Self, the earth will return to the paradise it has always been.

Chapter 5

Meditate Your Way to Good Health

"Health, a light body, freedom from craving, a glowing skin, sonorous voice, fragrance of body: These signs indicate progress in the practice of meditation."
—Upanishads

It is six o'clock on a winter's evening, the snow has finally stopped falling, and my kitchen is warm and inviting as I cook the evening's meal. In a moment, I will put on my boots and go out to shovel the walk for the students arriving shortly. For the past six weeks they have been following a rigorous practice of meditation and yoga while eating a whilefoods diet. I know the happy ending to each of their stories, having seen the results time and time again. The experience of feeling and looking great, while still able to cope with the stress of everyday life, has convinced these people that caring for themselves—mind, body, and spirit—has a major impact on how one feels, thinks, and acts. It is a simple practice that results in a clear, focused mind and a clean, healthy body.

The Buddha taught that you will know the results of your practice when you become aware of feeling joy, compassion, and loving kindness for yourself and all other sentient beings. This internal awakening is also reflected in the health of your body. As you become liberated from the mental afflictions, the physical cravings that accompany them subside as well.

The Physical Benefits of Meditation

"You can expect certain benefits from meditation. The initial ones are practical things; the later stages are profoundly transcendental. They run together from the simple to the sublime."

—Bhante Henepola Gunaratana

It may seem incredible that the health benefits garnered from a practice of meditation can occur just from sitting quietly, doing nothing, and watching what arises in your mind. Where there exists chaos and confusion, meditation brings calm and insight. The proper breathing of meditation increases the amount of oxygen to the brain, which soothes the nervous system and improves the circulation of blood.

In addition to contributing to better health, scientific research has shown a clear link between a regular practice of meditation and a longer life. With all the ways that come to mind for extending life, only two have been documented to work: restricting food calories and lowering one's core body temperature. Meditation can lower core body temperature.

Meditation has also been shown to aid in the prevention and cure of certain illnesses and addictions. The practice has been used successfully in the treatment of drug addiction, helping addicts to better cope in their recovery program.

Meditation also is used in psycho-neuro-immunology (PNI) to help control the immune system and manage stress and pain. For individuals who are forced to endure a life of chronic pain, it is not always as simple as taking medication to deal with the daily trauma and anxiety. Meditation might not stop the pain, but it can break the cycle of stress, bringing calm and relaxation to the taxed nervous system. Dr. Jon Kabat-Zinn, author of *Wherever You Go There You Are* and the director of the Stress Reduction Clinic at the University of Massachusetts

Medical Center, has been teaching mindful meditation to patients at his clinic since 1992 and has documented his results.

He found that 72 percent of the patients with chronic pain conditions achieved at least a 33 percent reduction after participating in an 8-week period of mindful meditation, whereas 61 percent of the pain patients achieved at least a 50 percent reduction. Additionally, these people perceived their bodies as being 30 percent less problematic, suggesting an overall improvement in self-esteem and positive views regarding their bodies. His studies also showed that when people with asthma, emphysema, and chronic obstructive pulmonary disease (COPD) learn breathing techniques associated with meditation, they have fewer respiratory crises, and that people with psoriasis who practice meditation saw the affected area of skin clear up more quickly.

As more and more researchers study meditation as a healing tool, doctors in many parts of the world have reported success in treating cancer, infertility, premenstrual syndrome, tension headaches, irritable bowel syndrome, ulcers, insomnia, and fibromyalgia. This can only be explained by meditation's ability to bring about feelings of deep relaxation, giving its practitioners a literal vacation from stress.

Physiological Benefits of Meditation

The list of positive benefits from doing meditation are numerous and cover a host of mental and physical afflictions.

The physical benefits of meditation include ...

- Relaxation, as measured by decreased metabolic rate and lower heart rate.
- Lowered levels of cortisol and lactate—two chemicals associated with stress.
- Reduction of free radicals, which are unstable oxygen molecules that can cause tissue damage.
- Lower blood pressure.
- Higher skin resistance. Low skin resistance is correlated with higher stress and anxiety levels.
- Drop in cholesterol levels. High cholesterol is associated with cardiovascular disease.

- Increase of oxygen to the lungs, resulting in easier breathing.
- Increased longevity.
- Higher levels of the youth hormone DHEAS in the elderly.

The psychological benefits of meditation include ...

- Increased brainwave coherence.
- Greater creativity.
- Decreased anxiety.
- Decreased depression.
- Less irritability and moodiness.
- Improved learning ability and memory.
- Increased self-awareness.
- Increased feelings of vitality and rejuvenation.
- Increased joy and happiness.
- Increased emotional stability.

A Healthy Body and Mind

The longer you practice meditation for health reasons, the greater the likelihood that your goals will shift toward personal and spiritual growth. Dr. Joan Borysenko, in her work with cancer and AIDS patients, has observed that many of them become interested in meditation as a way of becoming more attuned to the spiritual dimension of life, so they will be able to die feeling as if they were in a state of compassionate self-awareness and self-acceptance.

Overcoming Addiction

"Excess of sorrow laughs. Excess of joy weeps. Joys impregnate. Sorrows bring forth."
—William Blake

Many people in the Western world find they need some form of chemical prop to keep pace with our stress-oriented society. This temporary help may come from using substances such as alcohol, cigarettes, coffee, tea, or prescription or recreational drugs. Other addictive props include television, sugar, chocolate, exercise, gambling, dieting, shopping, or work. It takes tremendous courage to pick yourself up from the pits of hell and give up your addictions, but one proven way to get there is with meditation.

Suffering from attachment to something can include needing to have a cigarette or eat a piece of rich chocolate. In the process, the pleasure is all too quickly over, and before it is even finished you find yourself wanting another. You can feel—maybe even think—that you don't want it to end, because then you must have one more and then one more. When you try to rid yourself of your addiction, your body begins to withdraw from the effects of the drug, nicotine, caffeine, or sugar. You become irritable, when only a short time before you were happy to inhale the smoke, or let the chocolate melt in your mouth. Now you are suffering; instead of playing with smoking or eating, you are a smoker, you are a chocoholic; you identify with the label, and your attachment causes your suffering.

Of course, not all dependencies are life threatening, but they all affect your mind and body. Having a cup of tea after a hard day's work or the odd bar of chocolate is not a serious form of addiction. However, when you reach the point of experiencing panic, severe anxiety, or fear of being unable to cope without your tea, chocolate, alcohol, or cigarettes, you have a problem.

Recognize Suffering for What It Is

The Buddha taught that we "mistake suffering for happiness." Humans invariably find a way to ease the pain of lost pleasure, if only temporarily. We get hooked on things, whether food, alcohol, or exercise, because they offer a temporary relief and are so readily available. Done long enough, they become the heart of our existence and cannot be so easily given up.

The Transcendental Meditation Organization has done extensive research into the effects of meditation on the mind and body. Studies show that the use of Transcendental Meditation can help people reduce their use of alcohol, cigarettes, and nonprescription drugs. Over an 18 to 24 month period, abstinence rates ranged from 51 to 89 percent when using transcendental meditation, compared to only 21 percent for conventional substance-abuse programs.

Become a Spiritual Warrior

Meditation teaches us how to wait, to see something through to the end. Waiting requires patience and an internal stillness. To wait through our desires is what is called for from the spiritual warrior. A warrior accepts the challenges that life presents without complaint and strives to live a life of integrity and passion in each moment. The ancient Celtic oracle of divination, The Runes, say that "The battle of the spiritual warrior is always with the self. Finding a will through action, yet unattached to outcomes, remaining mindful that all you can really do is stay out of your own way and let the Will of Heaven flow through you."

Addictions are often a vain attempt to be present in the moment. People use them to forget the past by running away from previous actions and regrets. They use them to avoid their fear of the future either because it is empty or there is more harm to come. People use their addictions to try to hold on to an immediate pleasure that is a fleeting illusion.

The Pleasure-Pain Cycle

"Attachment is the mind stuck to an object."

—Lama Zopa Rinpoche

One morning as a student arrived for class with her five-year-old daughter, I noticed the child was very upset, her body tense and the look on her face showed fury. When she would not reply to my greeting I looked to the mother, who shrugged and said, "I wouldn't let her have a piece of chocolate." I could see that the little girl was showing all the symptoms of withdrawing from a drug, in this case sugar and caffeine. All she knew was that she needed to have what her body craved and she would experience pleasure again, but without it her mind and body was in a state of pain and discomfort.

The roller coaster of the pleasure-pain cycle can be as simple as dreading a cloudy day and feeling joyful when the sun appears. Men and women who move from one relationship to another are trapped in the cycle of wanting the pleasure of the initial romance and fear the pain of a cooling passion.

To fear physical pain is a nervous response on the part of our mind-body relationship. Psychological pain is the fear of losing what brings satisfaction, including money, family, and possessions. The accumulation of things, beliefs, opinions, and possessions creates a fear of losing them, which in turn would cause you pain. To keep what you have accumulated, you will need a way to protect it all. This requires an alarm system for your home, a powerful military for your country, or a handgun for your personal arsenal. As you see what is needed to sustain your pleasure-pain cycle you may find some comfort in knowing that you're not alone—it holds true for everyone else as well as yourself. Life's paradox is that so long as I want to have things in my life I need to protect, and as long as I have beliefs I need to defend, then I will always live in fear, and there will always be pain.

The question of attachment and desire is one of the most misunderstood things in the spiritual realm. Spiritual detachment means equanimity and evenness, an unconditional openness to everything. We all want to give up pain, but we don't want to give up pleasure; there's a problem there, because those two go together. Since each pleasure is impermanent it follows the cycle of changing to its opposite, pain, which flips us back to craving the pleasure once again. It's desire either way: We want what we want, and we want not to have what we don't want. It is equally wanting, demanding, craving, dissatisfying. We run our whole lives bouncing around on the pleasure-pain principle. "I want. I don't want." It's exhausting.

Practice

The only way to break the pleasure-pain cycle is through being mindful in your meditation. The human mind can be compared to a monkey leaping from tree to tree as our thoughts jump from one to another. Then there is the incessant chattering sound that certain monkey's make, which is much like our mind's speed-dialing of thoughts. This barrage of thoughts, images, movies, fantasies, emotions, and conversations is often called the "drunken monkey brain." When you step back to watch, you may be shocked by what you see.

Sit comfortably and bring your attention to your breath. Relax your shoulders and the tension in your jaw. Bring your attention to the fluctuations of your thoughts and observe how they spiral from pleasurable to painful images. In a matter of seconds, you can move from feeling good about someone or something to feeling sad or angry. Don't let the thoughts pull you in; make no judgments; just allow the breath to lead you in and out. Use the Pleasure-Pain mantra to help disconnect you from this repetitive cycle.

Pleasure-Pain Mantra

Breathing in, I watch the fluctuations of my mind

Breathing out, I see the duality of my nature.

Breathing in, I watch the fluctuations of my mind

Breathing out, I fill my heart with loving-kindness.

Get to know your pattern of pleasure and pain. By observing it over time, you will see how your actions affect others in your life. When the mind settles down, in that place of calm attention you will be able to see that what is revealed is the true nature of your heart.

Free and Easy: Reduce Stress

"You can only have bliss if you don't chase it."

—Bhante Henepola Gunaratana

Peter had been on the fast track of corporate life since he graduated from college. Shortly after joining the ranks of a major food company, he saw that his chances for advancement were small unless he had a masters degree. So, while his friends were out having fun on the weekends, he was home studying. Over the years, relationships with women came and went as success and promotion were his only priority. He took on one project after another, focused his mind on future goals, and accepted the stress as just part of the job. When he was in his 20s, he mentally lived for when he was 40—retired, rich, free to buy his land and settle down to the easy life.

At first he didn't give much thought to the minor aches and pains in his body; after all, he ran every day and ate moderately well. The drinking concerned him a little, but it was the only thing that helped him to settle down after a stressful day at the office. His stomach was causing him pain—an ulcer, his doctor told him. His sleep was erratic—he was up and down all night and he couldn't shut down his brain. The endless parade of thoughts were driving him crazy, and he had no idea how to make them go away. A friend told him how meditation had helped her deal with stress. She didn't mention how it had changed her life in other ways.

Stress is defined as a force that strains or deforms. This is obvious from the way it can twist the guts of your body and weaken your mental stability. It is a major factor in most people's lives—so much of one that many people take medication to help them deal with the anxiety it causes. Repercussions from too much stress can severely affect the body's ability to cope. It can weaken the immune system, making the body more susceptible to hypertension, heart disease, and a host of other ailments. Research has shown that hormones and other biochemical compounds in the blood indicative of stress tend to decrease during meditation practice. These changes also stabilize over time, so that a person is actually less stressed during daily activity, not just when meditating.

When Peter began to practice meditation, he came to understand how living in the nonexistent future had caused him to miss most of his life. He was basing his future happiness on when he would have enough money, the perfect woman, and a house he had built, and the stress to attain this goal was making him sick. Slowing down and being present to his thoughts made him realize that, as he reached his goals, he experienced no satisfaction, only more stress in his determination to reach the next one. Meditating helped him to dissolve the stress in his mind, and he was able to deal with the pressures at work, allowing his body to relax and heal.

Practice

Take a moment away from the hustle and bustle of your life and lay down on your back. Place a small pillow under your head so that your neck aligns with your spine. Let your feet open out to the sides and extend your arms, letting them rest on the floor or bed as a baby's would, slightly bent and away from the sides of the body. Close your eyes and bring your focus into your body. Silently recite the Relaxation mantra as you begin, with your toes (Breathing in, I relax my toes), letting go of any tension.

Slowly work your way up the body, relaxing your feet, legs, pelvis, lower back, belly, middle back, chest, upper back, shoulders, arms, hands, fingers, neck, jaw, tongue, cheeks, eyes, ears, and scalp, breathing out the tension and accepting the sense of peace that is left in its place. Stay present to what is happening—this is not a time to sleep, but to consciously create a concentrated state of deep relaxation.

Relaxation Mantra

Breathing in, I relax my ....
Breathing out, I am at peace.

Imagine that the floor is a giant sponge absorbing all the tension in your body and leaving you free and light as a feather. To conclude this practice, begin to smile, stretching the feeling around your entire body.

The Breath of Life: Breathe Easier

"If we train our breathing, we can control our emotions—that is, we can cope with the happiness and pain in our lives."
—Buddhadasa Bhikkhu

One common technique for breathing in meditation involves focusing on the inhale and exhale. Sometimes it is sequenced, sometimes counted, other times observed as it flows naturally, rising and falling without any effort on your part. The breath can be considered the key that unlocks the door to the inner Self. When you meditate regularly, you will find that you automatically bring your awareness to your breath whenever you need to calm or focus your mind.

I met a man once who told me how his quick temper had ruined his marriage and relationships with co-workers. Someone had suggested he try meditation to gain control over his emotions. What he found was that the angrier he became in a situation, the more his chest would tighten from holding his breath until he would explode with verbal or physical violence. He began to focus his awareness on just breathing calmly. To his surprise, his heart rate would begin to slow, the tension in the pit of his stomach eased, and he could take a full, deep inhale, dissipating his anger.

Another time, I noticed a woman who attended my yoga class was struggling with trying to coordinate her movements with her breathing. I went to her and asked her just to sit quietly and focus her attention on her breath. After the class she thanked me, saying that it had been a profound revelation to find that she was not breathing for long periods of time between breaths, that she was actually holding her breath! (Believe it or not, this is very common. When first practicing meditation, you may find that you hold your breath for a few seconds without even knowing that you do so.)

Godfrey Devereux, in his book *The Elements of Yoga,* describes how there is no amount of flexibility, strength, stamina, or concentration that can compensate for breath that is repressed in the body. If the breath is inhibited, the mind cannot free itself from limitations from past conditioning and old habits. The breath is the sherpa that leads the climber to the peak of Everest; it is the guide that lovingly takes us through the restrictions of our mind to the true nature of the Self.

Practice

Remember that the traditional practice of breath meditation is to simply sit still. Now close your eyes and center yourself to the flow of your breath. Slowly begin to count to six on the inhale, count to six on the exhale. Do this for six rounds. Take three normal breaths, and then count to six for the inhale and deepen the breath to eight on the exhale. (This takes you deeper into a state of relaxation). Do this for another six rounds. Take three normal breaths and return to a six-count inhale with a six-count exhale for six rounds. At the end of this, relax and breath normally. Remember that you are not the *breather* but rather the *observer,* watching the natural flow of each inhale and exhale.

Breath Mantra

Breathing in, I open my lungs.

Breathing out, I dissolve all thought.

This mantra helps you to be aware of breathing slowly and fully, one breath following another. Each exhale reminds you to let go of any thoughts trying to pull you away from your concentration, keeping you present to the moment.

Stress-Free Eating: Improve Your Digestion

"The secret to long life is a flexible spine and the digestion of a lion."

—Old yogic saying

A friend came to visit one spring and I was surprised by how much her skin had aged and how bloated her body looked. She told me how she had been under a great deal of stress from her job and was eating whatever she could grab in a hurry. Her doctor had diagnosed her as having inflammation of the large intestine called diverticulitis, but had not given her any guidance, other than medications, for her condition.

During her 10-day visit, I prepared fiber-rich organic vegetables and grains that were easy for her to digest, and I also got her started doing a morning meditation practice. I showed her how to guide her pranic (breath) energy into the lower half of her body and visualize her intestines as strong and healthy. By the time she left for home, the bloat had subsided, her energy had improved, and she was feeling at peace with herself. She continued her meditation practice, completely revamped her diet, and eventually healed her intestines.

A strong, healthy digestive system requires physical rest, mental calm, and fibrous foods. High amounts of stress can cause intestinal disorders by reducing the circulation of blood to the absorptive areas of the bowels. Meditation has been shown to aid in the treatment of many digestive problems, including colitis, irritable bowel syndrome, and gastric ulcers.

When the mind and body are under pressure, excess hydrochloric acid is released in the stomach and the core of the body becomes rigid with tension. Your digestive system is only reflecting what is going on in your mind, and what you are putting into your mouth. Both stress and refined, processed, sugar-laden foods create an acid condition in the digestive system. "Dis"-ease grows in an acid condition, whereas optimal health requires a more alkaline/acid balance. I compare it to how the afflictions of our thoughts create an acid mental condition. Meditation provides the alkaline balance to sooth and calm our internal ecology.

Here are some of the digestive benefits of meditation:

- Calms the stomach, reducing acidity
- Releases tension in the large/small intestine
- Helps the body absorb nutrients

Practice

Hand mudras are ancient healing techniques that an be used to improve physical, emotional, and spiritual health. The *Jnana mudra,* which I'll walk you through in this section, improves the digestive system, relieves internal stress, and guides pranic (breath) energy. In addition, this particular mudra directs energy to the lower abdominal area of the body.

Sit in meditation posture and rest a hand on each thigh. Cross the ends of your thumbs over the index fingernails. (It looks like you've made a circle with your finger and thumb). Close your eyes and observe your breath as it lifts your chest up and out on the inhale, descending deep into the lower abdomen on the exhale. Allow it to rise naturally without forcing the breath to happen.

Pay particular attention to the exhale, as you visualize a warm golden light moving around and through your pelvis. After you have made this connection in your mind, repeat the Energy mantra to focus your intention and create the link to your body.

Energy Mantra

Breathing in, I digest my food with ease.

Breathing out, I absorb all necessary nutrients.

The positive affirmation of the Energy mantra is received by both your mind and body, reaffirming the intention to transform illness or negativity into the possibility of optimum health and well-being.

Stand Tall: Change Your Posture

"Joyful steadiness in the body free from tension"
—Patanjali, Sutra II.46

You woke up early, lit the candle in your sacred space, sat on your cushion to meditate, and within minutes your back, ankles, or knees were screaming in pain. Welcome to the club. It will help if you take a few moments before sitting down to do a few side and forward stretches, just to open up the body a bit.

Each morning, I take the time to strengthen my core abdominal muscles as part of my meditation/yoga practice. This helps to support my back and provide an erect spine during long sits in meditation. Without this strength, your back will slump as you cave in to the pull of gravity, weak abdominals, and soft back muscles. This can be very uncomfortable and eventually will create stress between your shoulder blades and lower back. You can strengthen your abdominal muscles by practicing yoga or doing sit-ups. In addition, holding an erect posture in meditation will help to lift and align your body over time. In the beginning, you can sit against a wall for support or in a straight-backed chair; but it is this lift of the spine that you will need for comfort, and, most importantly, for your breath to flow freely without interference.

Over time, your practice of sitting with proper alignment will begin to show up in how you stand, walk, and sit throughout the day. Holding the body erect during meditation will become a part of your body's muscular memory, and you will maintain your posture without any mental effort or extra thought. This will give your lungs more room to expand, take pressure off your vital organs, and reduce the amount of wear and tear on your lower spine and back muscles.

Practice

Sit comfortably on a cushion with your legs crossed in front of you, or in a straight-backed chair, only this time stay seated forward toward the edge of the chair and not leaning against the back. Close your eyes and allow your spine to find its natural lift and alignment, keeping your shoulders relaxed and free from tension. Notice any tightness in your body from working to keep yourself in an upright position. Make a mental note where those places are located and bring your focus back to your body. Visualize your breath moving into those places that are tight from this holding, and use the ebb and flow of your breath to ease the tension there.

Now move your upper body from side-to-side, roll your shoulders a few times, and then come back to an upright position. Notice if you are leaning to the right or left and, when shifting yourself to align the spine again, notice what tension is caused to support this lift. Come back to the breath and direct its flow to the identified constrictions on your next exhale of breath. Repeat the Posture mantra to focus your mind on staying lifted through the core center of your body.

Posture Mantra

> *Breathing in*, I align my spine.
>
> *Breathing out*, I let go of tension.

The state of your body reflects the state of your mind. When your body is tense, so is your mind. Similarly, when your body begins to slump during meditation, you begin to lose your mental focus. With practice, you will be able to sit comfortably for longer periods of time with good posture and a relaxed, yet focused, mind.

A Thinner You: Lose Weight

"When you try to get rid of fear or anger, what happens? You just get restless or discouraged and have to go eat something or smoke or drink or do something else."

—Ajahn Sumedho

Sonia considered herself a member of the lifetime dieting club. She had been obese since childhood, having subsisted primarily on fast food and soda pop. As a teenager, she developed diabetes and, as she slipped into adulthood, her blood pressure rose out of bounds. She would wake up in the morning feeling like a truck had hit her, and it would take a few cups of coffee to get her moving at half speed. The stress on her heart and lungs had shortened her breath, her feet were swollen, and all her joints throbbed with a dull ache. On top of it all, she was having panic attacks and stopped going out into public. Then one day she turned on the television and happened to hear a Buddhist monk speak about meditation. He said that to lose weight all you need is to do nothing. She was amazed. What did he mean by nothing? He told his audience that when you are anxious and craving food as a distraction from the pain of your life, sit in meditation and wait and endure the restlessness. As you observe your mental conditions—the agitations, the emotional highs and lows, the judgments and criticisms—they will begin to ease up and dissolve in the light of your awareness. You will attain a kind of calm and mental clarity, which you will never achieve if you're always going after something else.

Sonia decided to try meditation for herself. She wrote down the monk's instructions and began to practice every day. She stayed through her restlessness, ignored all the excuses to stop, endured her self-criticisms of her overweight body, and one day understood that all those thoughts had nothing to do with who she was. They were projections from her past, illusions her mind had created. She'd had a glimpse of someone else behind the smokescreen of her negative thoughts, and she knew it would take patience to find that person.

As she practiced meditation, her mind became calm and peaceful. She was able to see how often she ate for no other reason than for something to do or because she felt depressed and thought ice cream would make it all better. During one meditation session, she remembered how, as a young girl, her father would take her out to eat ice cream. It was their special time together, and Sonia saw how she had been using the pleasure of her past experience to deal with her difficulties in the present. Having made this realization, she was able to stop using food to repress her emotions. She began to feed her body nutrient-rich foods and, little by little, the weight came off.

Practice

Each time you eat a meal or snack, ask yourself whether you are really hungry or just bored. When you crave a certain kind of food, take the time to note your frame of mind or mood and the associated craving in your journal. If you find yourself overeating stop yourself and sit quietly. As the craving builds, observe your thoughts, excuses, and demands to satisfy the desire. Repeat the Body mantra until you feel a sense of peace and the urge to eat has passed. Think of your breath as a feast that feeds every cell in your body.

Body *Mantra*

> *Breathing in,* I am satisfied.
>
> *Breathing out,* I dissolve all craving.

The breath feeds your body as the mantra feeds your mind, bringing needed peace and calm to your nervous system. Use this practice and take one to two weeks to slowly overcome your dependence on caffeine, alcohol, nicotine, or sugar.

On Eating Right

Put Your Mind on a Diet

People have known for centuries that the quality of the food they eat determines the clarity of their thinking, or in the case of meditation, not thinking. If your body is in a constant state of stimulation from drinking coffee or soda pop and eating sugar products, it will be very difficult to sit still for any length of time. The mind and body will be severely agitated, making it impossible to slow down the thoughts and bring a sense of calm to your meditation. On the other hand, a large meal, high in saturated fats and starches—let's say the standard American burger, fries, and milkshake—will make you so sleepy that you are more likely to nod off during your meditation.

Clean Body, Clear Mind

"If you want to progress on a spiritual path, you must challenge
your actions—including what you eat—as to whether they are
authentic expressions of the love and spirit within you."
—John Robbins

I have a friend who loves to collect clichés. He believes that we repeat
them so often because they have some truth to them. Take, for example,
the old adage "You are what you eat." Even more than that, you are
what remains in your body after the rest has been eliminated. Restricting
your food choices can be beneficial to your health, and can also serve as
an investigation into your true nature. The manner in which animals are
raised and slaughtered carries both energetic and karmic consequences
that the human race must all share. Compare it to standing by while
someone you love is being harshly abused. You wouldn't. You would
find a way to help them from being hurt or killed. We share the karma
because we are aware of the pain that is being inflicted and do nothing
to prevent it from happening. The ethical treatment of animals is the
responsibility of all peoples and is one of the precepts of right and moral
conduct to do no harm.

Empirical evidence shows that energy cannot be destroyed. The
energy we put into the preparation of our food, as well as, the energy
that remains in the fiber of the meat you eat, can affect how you think
and feel on any given day. With meditation, you bring a calm and tranquil mind to the kitchen, and the results of that mental energy is transferred to your food and back again to the body. Does this mean that
you must be a vegetarian in order to become liberated? People have been
considering this question since ancient times. The different schools of
thought range from strict vegetarians, who wear a face mask so as not
to accidentally swallow an insect and cause harm, to those who transform the karmic energy of slaughtered animals to a higher level and use
it for good. The range of beliefs and perceptions are wide and diverse
including whether to confine animals for their butter and milk or chickens for their eggs. Each individual must decide for him or herself.

I believe that a balanced vegetarian diet can help to calm and center
the body in tune to how meditation brings peace to the mind. Consum-
ing meat that still holds the animal's pain and fear does not contribute to

a calm and centered body; instead, it causes feelings of heaviness and lethargy. A diet made up of mostly meat, fish, eggs, overcooked and packaged foods can make a person dull, lazy, lacking in high ideals, purpose, and motivation. This can eventually result in developing chronic ailments and suffering from depression.

The standard American diet is high in refined flour products such as white bread, baked goods, and pasta. The problem here is that all the beneficial fiber and nutrients have been stripped from the grain leaving behind a dead food, oftentimes refortified with synthetic minerals. These refined flour products act as a glue to your intestines as there is no fiber that the intestines can use to stimulate peristaltic action. The result is chronic constipation, which can lead to a wide range of intestinal problems.

A friend of mine had to go to court for a divorce procedure and wanted to stay calm and centered so as not to be taken over by anger. The week before, he followed a simple diet consisting of vegetables, beans, sea vegetables, and grains, in combination with a daily meditation practice. He succeeded in staying relaxed and focused on one of the worst days of his life.

A Simple Vegetarian Menu

Here is what a typical day's worth of meals might look like if you took away meat, refined flour, and refined sugar products:

- **Upon rising.** Juice of half a lemon in 1 cup warm water with 1 tsp. raw honey (Prepares the digestion system)
- **Breakfast.** Cooked grain cereal with organic butter and maple syrup
- **Midmorning snack.** Handful of roasted almonds and raisins
- **Lunch.** Bean burrito with brown rice and mixed-greens salad
- **Afternoon snack.** Fruit smoothie made with your choice of milk product, banana, strawberries, and maple syrup
- **Dinner.** Vegetable soup, whole-grain bread, green salad

This is a very basic menu that you can enhance with a variety of organic food additions. It supports a clean, healthy body and a clear, focused mind. Of course, it always makes sense to check with your physician before changing your diet.

Being present to each moment includes the time you take each day to nurture your body and mind. Use the following practice to notice what occurs for you in the course of a day when sitting down to a meal. Then recite the Mindful Eating mantra silently in your mind to help guide you back to an awareness of eating mindfully.

Practice

Prepare your meal and sit at the table with nothing to distract you or take your attention from your food. Take a moment to give thanks for the abundance that has been provided to you from the universe. With each bite, close your eyes and stay in the awareness of chewing your food until it is liquid. Savor every mouthful, with full awareness of the texture and tastes in your mouth. Observe your reactions to the process of eating in this way. All digestion begins in the mouth, where the teeth masticate the food and the digestive enzymes are released from the salivary glands.

Sit quietly after you have finished, allowing the digestive system to continue its work without the stress of rushing off to the next project.

Mindful Eating Mantra

Breathing in, May all sentient beings have food to eat.

Breathing out, May all sentient beings cease to suffer.

Being grateful for what you have in your life and sharing your intention that others may be as fortunate leads to compassion and loving kindness.

It's All About You

The quality of your thoughts is strongly influenced by what you eat. To enhance your meditation, prepare your meals lovingly with your own hands, taking the time to ensure that your body receives the highest-quality nutrients.

Moving Meditation: Preparing Your Food

Learn to prepare your meals as a form of meditation. Soon you will look forward to each day's quiet time in the kitchen. The act of cooking requires focus and concentration, attention to detail, and a spontaneous creativity that springs from the heart.

For this practice, have a recipe you want to try or an idea in your head for some new taste you want to explore. Recite the Nourishing mantra to yourself when you notice your thoughts drifting in a negative way and again before you eat the meal. Music is always a welcome companion and can help keep you centered as you move from one task to another. Then, when the meal is ready, sit to receive the bounty of your actions, and recite the Nourishing mantra before you eat.

Cookbook for the Soul

The art of cooking, much like the practice of meditation, has an order to it that requires patience and a calm mind. It is a dance of timing as you put the grain on to cook, bake the squash, marinate the fish, chop the vegetables, and steam the greens. Cooking teaches you to nourish all your senses.

Nourishing Mantra

Breathing in With a clear mind, I nourish my body.

Breathing out With gratitude, I give thanks for this bounty.

Use the mantra to keep your mind free of negative thoughts. Let your positive mental energy be an additional ingredient you add to each recipe.

Guided Meditation: Healing Yourself

When you suffer from disease or illness, you can consciously support the healing process with this meditation and affirming mantra. The important thing is to clear the way for your body to do the necessary healing work. Follow a clean diet, get plenty of rest, practice breathing, and meditate to calm your mind and raise the quality of your thoughts.

Because we tend to mistrust ourselves, we depend on someone else to heal us rather than combining our inherent power with that of a skilled medical practitioner. Healing yourself on a cellular level takes time and patience. You can begin by becoming aware of the connection between your mind, body, and spirit through the practice of meditation. This particular guided meditation is also helpful for moving pain from the body.

Make a commitment to meditate in your sacred space at the same time each day. Use the flame of a candle to center and focus your attention. (You can stay seated or lie comfortably on your back for this practice.) Close your eyes and follow the movement of your breath, let all thoughts pass into the background as you become one with your breath. Step into the energetic river moving through your body and follow it to the location of disease. Place your right hand over the area (liver, ovary, lung, kidney, and so on). If your right hand is above your waist, rest your left hand on an area below your waist. If your right hand is below your waist, the left hand rests above the waist. Stay this way for up to 30 minutes, using the Healing mantra to calm and focus your mind.

Healing Mantra

> *Breathing in,* The power of healing energy flows through me.

> *Breathing out,* My bloodstream washes me clean of disease.

Your right hand is acting as an energy conduit, similar to jumper cables, helping to release blocked energy that has taken the form of pain or disease. You should begin to feel a pulse in the fingertips of one hand and then the pulse will switch to the other hand. When you feel the pulse in the fingertips of both hands you have moved the blocked energy. Continue to rest in this position for another five minutes, staying relaxed and breathing gently. You have just released stagnant energy and dispersed it throughout the body so it can move freely.

Chapter 6

The Artist Within: Awakening Creativity

"Creativity is harnessing universality and making it flow through your eyes."
—Peter Koestenbaum

Long before I began to meditate, I was an artist working my craft in several mediums. I understand now how working on a piece of art was a form of meditation. Submerged in the process of sculpting, painting, developing photographs, dancing, or writing, I was brought into the present moment as the channel for creative energy. I felt totally alive. Over the years when life offered me other avenues to explore, I would find a way to bring the creative process into what I was doing. In 1998 I bought an old schoolhouse in the country with the intention of teaching yoga and meditation classes. I knew there would not be enough time to paint pictures, because I would be painting a fence or building the meditation temple instead. Digging the earth for vegetables and flowers, I wove a labyrinth through the garden and around the trees, laying a path to follow in my walking meditation.

When I realized how much time it would take to establish my teaching practice, I decided that my home would be my work of art, and that I could use the rugs I collect in my travels to reflect my sense of color and texture. The walls of my bedroom awaken for me the warmth of Morocco, which is great on gray winter mornings. My meditation/yoga space stimulates and balances my chi energy with items that reflect the colors of the Chakras: red, orange, yellow, green, blue, indigo, and violet. My kitchen is painted a soft green to awaken my heart and feed me when the earth is covered in white.

In the Buddhist monasteries of Tibet and India, the young monks undergo three years of training in the art of making Mandalas—symbolic, cosmic diagrams that represent the inseparable nature of the physical and spiritual universe. They are used in the rituals of Tantric initiation and are constructed out of grains of colored sand. Mandalas are temporary, built of impermanent materials; and, after hours of painstaking labor, the artist deliberately destroys his creation. The sand is swept up upon completion of the initiation and poured into a nearby stream or river.

Meditation has been scientifically proven to enhance creativity, intelligence, memory, alertness, and to integrate left and right brain functioning. It has been shown to improve physical, mental, and emotional health. In a word, meditation is an invaluable tool to ensure that you are at your very best—every day. You may be getting a good night's sleep, but medical science has shown that this is not enough to alleviate the stress and fatigue of modern life. Fatigue and stress builds, keeping you from experiencing the real joy of creative living and working.

The act of creativity is inherent in all of human nature and is subject to the fundamental universal principle that all things are impermanent and subject to change.

Creativity as a Spiritual Practice

"Creativity is an experience—to my eye, a spiritual experience. It does not matter which way you think of it: creativity leading to spirituality or spirituality leading to creativity."

—Julia Cameron

Art is defined in *Webster's New World Dictionary* as human creativity. This need to create is an expression of our soul that reaches back to the very beginning of time. The ancient yogis called it *pakritti,* the universal energy that makes up all forms of matter. Creation is the cycle of birth, growth, and dissolution, a never-ending circle to which we are intimately connected. Creative energy is a spontaneous manifestation in the cycle that ultimately dissolves into the unmanifested source, the Absolute or Divine Creator. All creation originates from and ends with this Divine wellspring, the binding web being unconditional love, compassion, and wisdom. Our individual creative contribution to this process is often determined by how we see and think of ourselves and the world around us. The cycle of creation continuously makes itself present in our inner being and the external environment. In meditation you can observe how, as one thought begins, evolves, and ends, another is there to replace it—perhaps how a daydream follows a full story line from beginning, middle, and ending, or the planning of a day's activities takes you from waking to bedtime. Christian meditation asks that you transform thought into creative prayer, using what arises—your anger, sorrow, confusion, gratitude, and joy—to connect with the Absolute Divine source that created all life.

Meghann is one of my yoga students; at just 20 years old, she has taught me a few things about life. She was born an artist and has honed her craft since the moment she knew that creation was possible. I asked her how practicing meditation helped her with her creative process. She told me that to create you must have an understanding of what's around you, your relationship to it. There must be an observance, a sitting with, a presence, a corresponding dialogue, a reciprocal giving out and letting in, a letting go—then silence. Creativity requires a willingness to see to it that the connection that has always been there is finally recognized and given form, given symbolic identity. Art is a metaphor for life, and life is a metaphor for living. Art is a recognition, integration, and understanding of what it is to be human.

In a spiritual practice, recognizing "what has always been there" is the discovery of the true Self and our connection to all species. We begin to understand the need for balance between our individual nature and the community as a whole, between our narcissistic nature and our altruistic one. Understanding what it is to be human encompasses all the day-to-day chores, activities, play, situations, and conversations that require creativity, spontaneity, and imagination. Consider, for instance, the following day-to-day activities:

- Decorating your home
- Cooking a great meal
- Having creative sex
- Taking time to play
- Writing a letter
- Designing your wardrobe
- Exercising your body
- Doing the dishes

These simple actions can be boring, mundane chores or enlightening lessons in spiritual creativity. The Chinese proverb, "Before enlightenment chop wood, carry water; after enlightenment chop wood, carry water," reminds us that the path to liberation and freedom does not vary once we are there, but how we live each moment determines the quality of our life along the way.

We Are All Artists

> "Inside you there's an artist you don't know about ... Say yes quickly, if you know, if you've known it from before the beginning of the universe."
> —Jalai Ud-din Rumi

Early tribal cultures believed that each member of the community could express his or her creative nature according to his or her own talents. They all shared in the creation of beauty, whether beading an animal hide, tattooing their bodies, or sketching the hunt onto cave walls. No one person was considered a better "artist" over another. Nowadays we tend to distinguish between those with artistic skill and those without, and yet, within each of us there is the need to re-create with our hands what we see around us and that which springs from our imagination.

According to Dr. William Glasser, author of *Choice Theory,* we live our lives based on five basic needs that are a part of our genetic structure.

- **Survival.** The ability to care for yourself. Consists of food, shelter, safety, and reproduction.
- **Belonging.** Our need to love and be loved. Includes relationships, community, and giving and receiving affection.
- **Power.** The ability to achieve in life. To be competent, skilled, recognized, and listened to in your work and relationships. To have a sense of self-worth and self-esteem.
- **Freedom.** To feel free. To have independence, autonomy, have and make choices, and take control of the direction of your life.
- **Fun.** To experience pleasure, play, and laughter.

These needs are the general motivation for all that we do in our lives, and we must use our imagination and creativity to fill these basic needs.

Don't let the word *artist* throw you into a negative tailspin. Creativity is necessary at work, in play, and in your relationships with other people. You have been utilizing your imagination and creativity since the moment you were born. The focus of consistent meditating is to fully experience the NOW where you, the artist, will witness how the power of creative energy can be used to transform your life in positive ways.

Practice

Come into your meditation space or find a quiet place to sit comfortably. Have your journal nearby to write down any important insights. Begin your meditation by reciting the Creative mantra, giving yourself permission to open to an expanded sense of creative possibility. Sit quietly for a few moments, bringing your focus to your breath and calming your mental chatter. Recall your activities over the past day. Don't just mentally list them, but observe your actions. What did you do with those 24 hours? Notice how you dealt with each situation in a creative manner. If you were operating from habit or afraid to move forward, ask yourself why you were blocked and observe the thoughts, excuses, and truths your mind provides. Take a moment to write in your journal what these creative blocks were, and then come back to meditation.

Creative Mantra

Breathing in, I give myself permission to be more creative in life.

Breathing out, I give myself permission to manifest my creativity.

To increase your level of creative energy, you must change your perceptions of yourself, your beliefs, and even your value system. Self-realization can come only with consistent practice over a long period of time. Be patient and the creative juices will flow.

Freeing the Artist Within

"Whatever you dream you can do, begin it. Boldness has genius, power, and magic in it. Begin it now."

—Goethe

The question is this: How can you become more consciously creative in all aspects of your life? Here are six suggestions for you to practice while sitting in meditation.

Identify your creative blocks.

Many people link the idea of creativity with artists, translated as "weirdos." Just because you don't dress strange, dye your hair blue, or pierce your tongue doesn't mean you cannot be creative. Others simply fear being judged, ridiculed, or laughed at. I tell my students not to worry about what others are thinking because they are just as worried about what you are thinking about them. As you identify your blocks, make a list in your journal of all the different ways you hold yourself back. This can include how you dress, your hairstyle, what color you paint your house, the kind of car you buy, what photographs you take ... you get the idea.

Change your perception of how things can be done.

When we go along seeing a situation the same way all the time, we develop mental blinders that limit our ability to dance with possibility. Carlos Castenada wrote that you must "learn to see, and then you'll know that there is no end to the new worlds of our vision." If you want to write a book, but consistently listen to your negative excuses, then, while in meditation, allow your perspective to change. Look at the situation with a positive attitude and ask yourself what you will need just to get started. (I need to open up some time, a pen and paper, and a quiet space [if not at home, then at the library].) No more excuses. Rather than see the distant future or frightening outcome, stay in the present and begin.

Focus on the positive aspects of your creative power.

You will generate more quality ideas by thinking positive thoughts than by putting yourself down and saying "no" all the time. How many people have you met who, when given a suggestion, say "no" before they even stop to think about what you just asked them? They can't help it, negativity is so deeply ingrained in their psyche. Are you one of those people?

When observing your thoughts in meditation, notice how many times you use the words *can't* (as in, I can't do it), *don't* (as in, I don't know how), *won't* (as in, I won't take the time), and *no* (as in, no it's too hard). Then go back and replace them with the words *can, do, will,* and *yes.* Just by shifting from the negative to the positive, your whole energy will change for the better.

Believe in your ability to manifest your creativity.

There are moments on the path to liberation when it feels like you are a spiritual being trapped in the wrong body and living someone else's life. Internally, your doubts and fears are waging war, and all you can remember is someone once telling you that your creative talents are zero and that you should forget about being an artist. So what do they know, anyway? Jazz great Charlie Parker once said that "Music is your own experience, your thoughts, your wisdom. If you don't live it, it won't come out your horn." In other words, only you can determine what you can and cannot do.

Give yourself permission to be more creative.

I have a friend named Annette who designs unique playing cards depicting women giving themselves permission. One says *Permission to love and accept yourself,* another says *Permission to feel joy,* another *Permission to express your own unique style.* Sometimes it's like that. We just need to give ourselves permission to do the most simple of things. As you sit in meditation, go ahead and give yourself permission to be a free and creative soul. Don't be surprised if the inner voice replies, "I knew that before you did, knucklehead."

Get out to creative places.

Whenever I am in need of inspiration, I head out to the city for an afternoon of museums, art galleries, or even bookstores. I bring along a small notebook, and occasionally I bring colored pencils, and make notes or draw sketches of what I see. It could be a certain shape or color that gets me thinking about a new idea, or maybe just the way cars line up in traffic. I look to see what people are wearing, I read the graffiti on the walls, and I listen to the sounds of civilization. A new restaurant always awakens my creative juices, as I anticipate the possibility of new tastes and textures and then experience them. I take all of this back home with me and sit with it in meditation. I watch it all come together in a swirl of input from what I call my creative adventure, and then I begin to work.

Surround yourself with creative people.

Being with creative people is a great motivator. Consider taking a course in creative writing, acting, ceramic making, or photography. Not only will you be in a venue that will encourage you to create, you'll also be around others tapping into the universal ocean of ideas and imagination.

Letting Go of Fear

"Fear is a natural reaction to moving closer to the truth."
—Pema Chodron

The major creative blocks we all face are the fear of failing, the fear of making a mistake, and the fear of stepping into the unknown. That unchartered, unknown territory, for many, is a place mined to go off in unpredictable ways. It can also be a dangerous place when meditating. You start out thinking your practice will bring you some relief from stress, but then you see the reality of impermanence. Nothing is known or certain in life. You start to ask yourself "What if I make a wrong move, slip, fall, crash to the earth?" Then, instead of taking the risk, you decide it is better to stay in your zone of comfort and just not move at all.

Buddhist nun Pema Chodron says you must get to know your fear, look it straight in the eye. Let your fear help to liberate you from old ways of seeing and thinking about your life. It takes tremendous courage to confront what scares you; but rather than flee, consider yourself lucky to have an opportunity to hold yourself in a place of love. With love comes understanding and acceptance. In this way you give creativity a space to grow from love, freeing you to share your creative gifts with the world. When you confront your fears, you are rewarded with profound insight and a renewed passion for what is possible. Creating out of love allows for compassion when mistakes are made, and also allows us to learn from those mistakes without judgment.

My friend Bill Goodwin has been teaching young people the art of jazz drumming for more than 30 years. He tells his students to relax and let go of any preconceptions. This advice applies equally well to all creative endeavors. Don't try to make something happen; instead let something happen. You must detach yourself. Don't qualify your thoughts. Let your art become a form of meditation.

Creativity and meditation require continuous practice; with time you get better and better eventually separating you from the technique.

When you find yourself stopped by fear, stay with it, watch it. Observe how the fear affects your thoughts, how it creates tension in your body (stomach churning, perhaps). The Shaiva Tantras, a set of yogic tests from the ninth century, say all that appears in your mind is consciousness, a form of mind energy. All your thoughts and emotions, positive and negative alike, come from the same substance and they are so fleeting that they can evaporate instantly, yet are powerful enough to create an inner reality you falsely identify as your Self. Secrets of Tantric meditation reveal that if you can recognize all thoughts as being mental energy, they will dissolve and no longer trouble you.

Practice

Sit quietly and focus on your breath. Bring to mind a creative project you have been wanting to complete or start but have been afraid to do so. Watch the fear—and the excuses that come with it—arise. Does the emotion have to do with something that happened in your past or something you visualize happening in the future? Bring your awareness to your breath and surrender to the present moment. It is in this space that the past or future can have no hold on you.

Recite the Fear mantra, with each inhale and exhale bringing calm to your mind and body.

Fear Mantra

Breathing in, I accept my fears.

Breathing out, I let them dissolve.

Often after we actually identify what frightens us, we can see how insignificant those frightening things really are. We see how they have no substance in the present moment. Letting go of fear frees the creative energy.

Creativity in Business

"Through meditation and by giving full attention to one thing at a time, we can learn to direct attention where we choose."

—Eknath Easwaran

For businesses to stay competitive, they must constantly generate new ideas, products, and services, and offer fresh solutions to problems. This requires maximum creative output from each member of the company. Ideas are a dime a dozen, the truly great ones all too rare. The stress and tension caused by this challenge to perform in the marketplace can directly work against what you are attempting to achieve. Here is where fear of failure can rear its ugly head and bolt your feet to the ground.

Major corporations and businesses around the world are using meditation techniques to relieve employee stress and bring clarity to overworked minds. Transcendental Meditation teaches a simple program of two 10-minute sessions, one in the morning and one in the afternoon, to rejuvenate body and mind. *Vipassana,* which means to see things as they really are, is one of India's most ancient techniques of meditation. Over the past 10 years, the technique of Vipassana has been extremely well received within the upper echelons of business, proving very useful in enabling business people to deal with stress, awaken creativity, and integrate principles of ethics and basic spiritual values into their daily business practices.

Practice

Before you begin your workday, take a moment to turn off the ringer on your telephone, close the office or classroom door, and close your eyes. Focus your attention on your breath and recite the Stress-free mantra silently to yourself.

Stress-Free Mantra

Breathing in, I calm my mind.

Breathing out, I relax my body.

Make a commitment to do this for 10 minutes before and right after work. You will be amazed how this simple technique will help to center and energize you for the entire day.

Identifying the Inner Critic

"Every time you don't follow your inner guidance, you feel a loss of energy, loss of power, a sense of spiritual deadness."

—Shakti Gawain

You've heard that voice before, the one that shows up uninvited and lets you know just how inadequate you are. ("Did you really think that idea was any good?" "How could you have been so stupid?" "You call that art? Looks like kindergarten work to me.") And I sound polite compared with the mind-lashing some of you give yourselves. The inner critic is alive and well, always close by to help keep you from moving forward. Yet in some cases, despite or maybe even because of our critic, we do move forward, overcoming great obstacles to, as Shakespeare says, "give to airy nothing a local habitation and a name." Some people give their critic a special name for immediate identification. My good friend Patty, an actress and businesswoman, calls hers Jezebel (or Jezzy, for short). Jezzy will show up to sabotage a performance, a business deal, or any attempt to have a loving relationship. We've laughed about her inner critic so many times over the years that I now ask when we speak by telephone how Jezzy is doing. The inner critic may have grown up with you, wearing the face of your mother or father. One artist I know told me that no matter what she did, it was never good enough. In her family, the competition was so fierce for her parents' attention that the praise went to the one who showed the greatest promise to be a doctor. Creative talent was deemed insufficient for making a living as an adult. It's no wonder her inner critic is forever telling her that she's not good enough to make a living with her artistic talent.

Our soul's purpose is to evolve toward our highest spiritual consciousness. No small order when getting yourself out of bed some mornings can be a major event in your day. Too often we settle for mediocrity because that is what is being fed to us through the media and from our own inner critic.

Letting Go of Judgment

"Being mindful means being fully absorbed in the moment, leaving no room for anything else. We are filled with the momentary happening, whatever it is—standing or sitting or lying down, feeling pleasure or pain—and we maintain a nonjudgmental awareness, a 'just knowing.'"

—Ayya Khema

I've made it a habit to be aware of myself when I'm being judgmental. I've gotten pretty good at catching my subtle remarks about myself or someone else. Then there's what I call the "Big J," the not-so-subtle comments that leave me somewhat shocked by my arrogance. When I find myself playing God like this, I say to myself, "Judging," and most of the time the thought dissolves instantly; other times I have to say it a few more times before the critic is quiet. My meditation sessions made me aware of how judgmental I can be. I was so taken aback at first that I started to laugh. It was as if I was watching some caricature of myself doing a stand-up comedy routine.

The judgments that you make about yourself have nothing to do with the truth. Those judgments come from your inner critic and are there to block you from reaching your goals. I call them "life's catch-22." The beauty of life is that it's a treasure hunt, and finding your true self is the grand prize. To find yourself, you must be totally present in each moment. When you sit in meditation with your mind centered, your gaze within, there is no space for judgments and criticism. When you are being mindful, there is no room for anything else but your total awareness of the moment.

Practice

Close your eyes and sit comfortably, letting your thoughts dissolve in the presence of your breath. Allow the image of yourself to arise in your mind and observe what your thoughts and emotions speak about you. Do you appear as two different people—the one you project to the outside world and they onto you, and the person you are within? Are these two images of yourself the same person or are they conflicted and opposite in nature? Notice how you speak to yourself, the judgments that your mind makes, any comments about your actions or fears. (For example: *That was stupid. Good going, knucklehead. You're an idiot.*) Observe how you judge yourself when emotions arise; do you view them as weakness or are they the natural release from your mental afflictions. In between the thoughts, bring your focus back to the breath, reciting to yourself the first line of the Judgment mantra on the inhale, the second line on the exhale.

Judgment Mantra

Breathing in, I soften my heart.

Breath out, I let go of judgment.

Observing your judgments and criticisms separates you from the inner critic and dissolves the illusion of your false self. Repeating the Judgment mantra helps you let go of the need to judge and criticize yourself.

A Date with Your Inner Artist

"If you never try, you can never be successful, but if you try, you might surprise yourself."

—Lama Thubten Yeshe (*The Bliss of Inner Fire*)

So now you have the choice to either indulge your passion for suffering or take a courageous stance in the practice of mindful awareness. The Dalai Lama says to just make a decision and act on it. Live in your negative afflicted mind or open to a whole new way of seeing yourself and the world. You don't have to go out and change your job, friends, or aspirations—for these areas of your life are exactly where you need to begin. Start right where you are. Begin to include compassion and loving kindness in your creative practice. Set aside one day a week to spend your time being creative. Make a commitment to use that time to explore new artistic avenues of expression or to work on the ideas you've been storing up in your mind. The following suggestions will help you along the way:

- **Keep a daily journal.** Julia Cameron, in her book *The Artist's Way,* suggests that you write three pages every morning, about anything that comes to mind. This can be considered a form of meditation practice because it helps to unblock your creative energy and clear your mind for the day ahead. You can also use your meditation journal to write any creative ideas and insights when they appear.

- **Let go of tension by indulging in a massage or body energy treatment.** After external tension has been eased, you can actually get in touch with what you are feeling.

- **Spend an afternoon at the bookstore or library.** This can be a very inspiring date with your inner artist, spending time reading books on the practice of meditation, art, and creativity. Make notes in your journal of things that stimulate creative ideas.

- **Take time to daydream about your creative ideas.** Daydreams can be a tool for your creativity when they consist of quality thoughts and intentions. Watch that your mind doesn't get bogged down in the frivolous and negative.

- **Begin to think of yourself as a creative person.** Support your creative identity by carrying through on creative projects and placing yourself in creative environments. Don't allow others to distort your perceptions by taking what they say personally. Accept that everyone will have an opinion and it has nothing to do with you.

- **Create the perfect creative space.** Nurture your creativity by creating a comfortable environment in which to play and have fun. Transform a room or corner where you can get away and bring your ideas to fruition. Take a moment before you begin and meditate. This helps to clear your mind and bring your creative ideas into complete focus.

Calling Upon Your True Self

In your meditation practice, keep your focus moving inward past the critical mind and the boisterous ego toward a place of stillness. The more you get to know the negative mind traps, the less power they will have. You will come to find your creativity beneath all the petty weakness and tyranny. Meditation is the form in which your creative self is mirrored back when you are quiet long enough to see the truth.

Practice

Whenever I need to break out of my rut, I put on some music and dance, even if it's in the middle of the day. Dancing gets all my body parts moving and allows me to disappear back into myself. You might think of this as active meditation, where the mind is stilled by the movement of the body. I also use my Hatha yoga practice—a form of active meditation—to change my energy and open a space for creativity to show up. No matter the size of your space, move the furniture up against the wall and put on some music that gradually builds from a slow and easy rhythm to a variety of tempos.

Begin by standing with your eyes closed, listening to the music. Bring your focus to your breath, allowing your mind to calm and center. Lift your arms up over your head on the inhale and lower them on the exhale. Continue with other parts of your body, trying to time the movement to the length of each breath. Roll one shoulder in a circle, and then the other. Bend your knees and round down to touch the floor, then raise back up again. As your body warms to the movement and begins to pick up the cadence of the song, let your body sway in time. From here just follow what your body feels it needs to do. You can stand in one place swaying, rolling, and lifting or dance around the room, leaping and cavorting. Give your creative spirit free rein to unleash its pent-up energy. Say or sing the Joyful mantra in your mind, or out loud, filling you with joy and laughter.

Joyful Mantra

Breathing in, I am free to fly.
Breathing out, I am free to soar.

Breathing in, Moving in my body
Breathing out, Opens my creative door.

So much of our creative stagnation comes from blocked energy. Mindful dancing is active meditation, where the mind is stilled by the movement of the body. Hatha yoga trains the mind to focus as the breath, body, and mind synchronize their movements. This is an excellent practice for opening a space in which creativity can emerge. There are a number of CDs on the market designed to accompany a moment of ecstatic dancing. Keep a few in your collection for just such a moment as this.

Creating in the Moment

"All the arts we practice are apprenticeship. The big art is our life."

—M. C. Richards

You cannot force yourself to be creative. Meditation teaches you patience with yourself. I often remind myself of an uncooperative child who is cranky and just doesn't want to play. I know I should be writing or painting, but the inner child would rather go for a walk or cook a meal. I find it best not to resist the flow, and instead use the time to mentally create what I am going to say or do. I always keep my journal handy for making quick notes in between stirring the soup.

Like meditation in motion, our awareness of the moment melts all resistance by staying with what is immediately called for. Seeing that each action is creation, the mind gives up resistance without a struggle. Your mind gently shifts its focus back to the task at hand, wasting no time in a draining struggle. With practice you are less likely to be pulled away from your creative flow, without having to push anything away: the resistance is allowed to simply dissolve on its own. This awareness can transform conflict, life stress, and even guilt. Starting a project, engaging a new idea, and giving yourself to the creative process becomes easier. Resistance is replaced by more and more calm as you stay in the flow of the present. You more freely surrender and engage with your art form or other activity, moment by moment.

Moving Meditation: Creative Freedom

Find an activity that interests you, whether it is painting a picture, arranging a bouquet of flowers, or decorating a room in your house. Take time to sit and contemplate what you would like to see in that space.

Close your eyes and allow yourself to feel what it is you would like to express as the final outcome. See it all clearly in your mind's eye and, when you have the vision before you, either sketch the design or write down a full description of it. Begin to work with a single-minded focus on what you have already seen.

Recite the Creation mantra to keep you present to the task at hand.

During the creative process, the actual work may change and shift, and new ideas awaken as you define your creation more clearly in your mind. Allow yourself to flow in the direction your creative instincts lead you. Give yourself enough time to accomplish either all or part of your creation. Take several days, if necessary, returning to the project with the clear intent that no other activities will disrupt your focus. Use this creative outpouring in addition to or in place of your daily sitting practice.

Creation Mantra

>*Breathing in,* I open to my imagination.
>
>*Breathing out,* I release all restrictions.

Try to let go of all judgments of good or bad, worthy or unworthy, about what you are doing. Know that whatever pours from your creative mind is inspired by the Divine presence of the true artist residing in your Self. This is a good time to observe how you interact with this creative being. Enjoy the process.

Guided Meditation: Unblocking Your Creativity

When it is difficult to contact your creative muse, take a moment to sit in meditation and listen for the voice of inspiration. So often it is hard to hear yourself think because of events in your life or distractions of the mind. Everything you need to know is already there, just waiting for you to quiet down long enough to notice.

Bring your focus to the exhale, following how it descends deep into your lungs. As you inhale, visualize a door opening, as if the wind blew it open. On the next exhale, allow all the debris of negativity stored behind the door to come flying out and dissolve in your gaze. Continue with this practice until the room is empty and nothing appears as you breathe. Now look into the room and see what is there. A thought, an image, a color, a word—take it in the exhale and bring it to life, as if it were a small ember. Stay present to what appears. Use the Inspiration mantra to keep you in the present moment. Stay with the process of bringing forth creative life, stopping if you need to write down your insights in your journal.

Inspiration Mantra

Breathing in, I open to inspiration.

Breathing out, I am filled with creative spirit.

Ask for what you want from the universe and it will gladly provide you with what you need. Remember that you are in partnership with the true Creator, and when you allow yourself to tap into some of that power, the creative energy will flow like a water hydrant uncapped.

Chapter 7

Great Sex and Deep Love

"To love is to return to a home we never left, to remember who we are."
—Sam Keen

What can the practice of meditation tell us about the true nature of love? Can sitting in silence and letting go of our thoughts make it possible to know real love in a culture obsessed with external beauty? Is great sex only to be found in the thrill of those first moments of lust and desire, or can practicing meditation guide us forward into a deeper more satisfying sexual experience? Joy, happiness, and pleasure are what everyone wants and deserves to have in his or her life. They can be easily found in the beginning of a relationship, and they can be maintained over time if a couple is willing to change and evolve together.

Opening the Road Blocks

"To love pleasure takes little. To love truly takes a hero who can manage his own fear."

—Clarissa Pinkola Estes

It is in the stilling of your thoughts that you begin to understand how you live with a constant chatter of opinions, beliefs, and negative emotions. These are the roadblocks you create day after day that prevent yourself from opening to the full realization that humans are not separate from each other, but intricately interconnected. Our feelings of separation stem from our ego's resistance to impermanence and change. To the ego, life is essentially, "all about me," and it creates isolation out of fear and distrust of others.

If you let your mind be filled with the thought that the act of sex is merely to derive physical pleasure for yourself, for example, it will be very difficult to understand your partner if he or she views it as an expression of love and intimacy. Holding on to a belief that love causes pain, rather than seeing love as a possibility for joy and happiness, will keep you from moving forward in any relationship. Fear can sabotage your attempts to open to a loving relationship, and your expectations of finding the perfect mate can cause you to miss the full pleasure of lovemaking as you mentally judge what you see as flaws in a person.

A daily practice of meditation allows time to train your mind to see how, in holding on to these mental afflictions, you are preventing yourself from being present to the joys of experiencing a fulfilling sexual life and to the opportunity to find true love.

When love shows up, it is unexpected, something that comes along and takes us by surprise. As the newness wears off, we begin to notice faults and weaknesses that don't jive with our picture of what we thought we wanted. The first shift has occurred, but rather than run away and look for the next bit of excitement, the challenge is to stay and see it through. Life is always changing, so why not go with the flow of its endless possibilities?

Interestingly, people experience this same instinct to flee when they meditate. While sitting on the cushion and watching the dark emotions arise, the tendency is to run, get up, do something—anything—rather than stay and deal with what is emerging from the cauldron of our minds.

In both love and meditation, we want only the good things, the pleasurable feelings, the excitement of new discovery; and why not, we deserve to have fun, right? But there's a limit, and too often we exceed that limit. Suffering happens when we get greedy and grab for more than we need, when we stay long after the party is over. Maintaining joy and happiness amid constant fluctuation is what the practice of self-realization is all about.

Patience and Right Intention

In our fast-paced culture, we expect the results of our practice to happen immediately. We want it now, yesterday, or at least in two weeks. If you're frustrated to find that after spending 20 minutes sitting on a cushion you still have trouble committing to one person in your life, don't be surprised. It requires patience with yourself, patience for learning what it takes to fully love, and patience when following your practice. Meditation is a commitment to awaken your higher consciousness, and it is one that extends throughout your lifetime. It is a returning to innocence, getting rid of the old ways of seeing, scraping off the barnacles, and perceiving space where it is possible to love someone and be loved in return.

At the heart of our world is an endless compassionate love greater than any you could ever imagine. When we meditate, we tap into that love. We come away with a tiny piece of it every time we sit and connect with this power greater than ourselves. Like water flowing over stones, practicing meditation over time wears away the negative emotions. As our hearts open, our minds also open to seeing the reality of each moment as it is happening.

When asked what the secret of her successful 30-year marriage was, my friend Laurie shared the following insight:

> Being willing and able to see that you are not going to get what you want from the other person, accepting them for who they are, and letting go of your expectations of who they are and making peace with yourself. It is important to make sure that your soul's need is covered rather than making a compromise

that is a violation to your soul. It also helps if there is chemistry between the two of you, but friendship and love are integral for the relationship to survive over time.

You may wonder how meditation can enhance your sex life, foster greater intimacy in relationships, and make you a more loving and compassionate partner and friend. It is simply because it provides clarity to a cluttered and distracted mind. One of the biggest gifts you can give yourself, your loved ones, and the world around you is to commit to a meditation practice right now.

Practice

Look over the following questions and then take a moment to sit in silence. As you mentally ask the questions below, observe the answers that appear in your mind. This is not a test, but a way to focus your awareness on your true motives and intentions when dealing with someone you think you love or someone you are in a casual relationship with. It can be difficult to be honest with yourself, but try not to defend your answers with judgments about others—the responses should focus on your thoughts and feelings about yourself. When you have observed the thoughts that arise, recite the Self mantra silently with each inhale and exhale:

- Do you demand sex from your partner as an escape from the tedium of your life, or is the act a mutual sharing of pleasure between the two of you?
- Do you use sex to control your partner, giving when you want something and refusing in order to punish him/her?
- Do you hold back and create distance out of a fear of what someone will think of you?
- Do you use a show of affection or love to get what you want from another?
- What emotions arise for you when it is time to make a commitment with someone else in a relationship?

Self Mantra

Breathing in, I watch my fears arise.

Breathing out, I let them pass away.

There are no right or wrong answers to these questions because they embody all the mindsets that are inherent in human beings. Knowing your ways of using others for self-gratification, and their ways of using you, is a first step toward creating positive change in your life. Watch any resistance that might arise to giving up your ego's need for control. Let the power of your breath and the mantra clear the way.

In the Beginning

"Fulfillment of desire is an illusion; desire leads to more desire, not satisfaction."

—Kathleen McDonald

The sexual desire we all seem to experience is a result of our instinctual nature to survive as a species. The problems arise when this desire is satisfied, the sexual attraction subdued, and the veil of illusion we use to see the world is lifted.

This early form of desire—a superficial form of love—is a self-centered emotion arising from our still-primitive instincts. We sometimes allow this desire to fill in for our lack of deep love. Because it is so exciting and pleasurable, we try to hold on to it, hoping it will last forever. Deep love develops over time only and cannot be rushed. It requires selfless giving and a compassionate nature, which are often overshadowed by our insecurities, our need for control and power, and our fear of opening up ourselves to someone else.

In the calm of meditation, the peace of mind you experience is as if a window has opened, bringing a fresh breeze of insight to your crowded brain. This helps you to see your partner with compassion and understanding, to accept him or her as is, and to treat your partner with the love and consideration you would wish for yourself.

Practice

Take this moment to close your eyes and sit in silence. Focus on your breath and observe how your thoughts battle for your attention. Don't try to stop them; instead, notice what they reveal to you.

Perhaps you had an argument with your partner, the same one you always have, the one that comes up over and over again and which you never seem to resolve. Perhaps it's the one about wanting more sex, but your partner is too busy or too tired; or maybe you're bored with the same old ways and would like to try some new sexual positions, but your lover doesn't want to.

You feel angry and resentful. Your mind is on a search-and-destroy mission, mentally reducing your lover to shreds. Notice whether your thoughts are about blaming the other person, about your need to be right in the situation, or how to get back at your partner for hurting your feelings.

This is your mind talking, judging, criticizing, attached to what you wanted to happen. This is your ego self, that part of you who is afraid of losing the primal desire that was once a part of the relationship.

Let the anger come up so that you can see its full force, its destructive nature. Watch how much tension and stress is caused by holding on to this emotion. It's natural to get angry when you feel threatened and vulnerable, but holding on to the negative emotion only blinds you to the possibility of seeing another way through the problem.

At this point, you might want to get up and run away, but stay and observe what is happening. Stand back and listen to what your ego is ranting about. In between thoughts, focus on your breath, taking in and letting go.

Use the Letting Go mantra to release your attachment to your opinion, your need to be right, and find that moment of emptiness between thoughts to rest from the chaos of your mind. In this moment of your life, just be with what is. If you are not attached to the outcome, there can be no disappointment or suffering.

Letting Go Mantra

Breathing in, I let go of being right.
Breathing out, I release the need to blame.

As you recite the Letting Go mantra with each breath, notice how your mind continues to make its points, but it becomes like an echo heard in the distance, like annoying background music. Stay with the mantra and, little by little, the tension will ease, the thoughts will recede further and further until they dissolve themselves in the light of your focus on letting go and surrendering.

Obstacles in Our Path

The entertainment media would have us believe that what is portrayed on television and film is the way of the world. Violence, sexual abuse, and an "anything goes" agenda leaves us jaded to the shock and horror of what we see. What was once considered evil is now commonplace and accepted in many parts of society. Fashion dictates that a woman, by nature round and curvaceous, be tall and rail thin, while men's magazines promote a buffed, hairless physique that few men can hope to attain. Rather than recognize and accept our bodies for what they are, we strive to mold them into a form that does not and will never fit who we are. As we are constantly bombarded with images of how we must look, eat, and act, how then do we come back to a place of stillness and retrain the mind and emotions to seek peace and compassion?

Changing old habits can be difficult at first, especially when you need to enlist the help of others in your endeavor. With the understanding that nothing is permanent or forever, use this next practice as a way to reestablish a connection with your partner, opening doors of communication that might have been closed unconsciously.

Practice

Make a commitment to yourself and your partner to turn off the television and not watch it for a week. If you typically spend time on the computer in on-line chat rooms or adult entertainment websites, avoid these as well. Instead, use this time to reacquaint yourself with your lover by preparing meals together, mindfully listening to how his or her day has been, or sharing your insights into your self. Invite your lover to sit with you quietly and meditate together. Being together in this way will help your to notice how the constant distraction of external forces pulls you away from what is most precious and necessary in your life and, with each other's likes and dislikes in mind, create a plan that will help to diminish these distractions so you have more quality time together.

Peace Mantra

As you sit together in meditation, say the first line of the Peace mantra in your mind on the inhale, the second line on the exhale, the third line on the inhale, and the fourth on the exhale. This is a powerful mantra to help you focus on a single thought, allowing all other thoughts to pass by:

Breathing in, My eyes open and I see you as you are.

Breathing out, My ears open and I hear what you say.

Breathing in, My heart opens and fills with love.

Breathing out, I am alive to what is happening in this moment.

Face your partner and, looking into each other's eyes, repeat the mantra to each other. Let the feelings of joy and love move through your body, coming to rest at your heart. Place your hands over each other's heart and feel the life pulse of your lover moving from his/her heart to meet yours.

Now take this union of energy and move into the bedroom. Light some candles to prepare for an intimate session of lovemaking. Begin by holding each other in a loving embrace, and then slowly explore each other's bodies with soft, gentle strokes of your hands. In the rush to reach orgasm, we often forget how important a soft touch can be on the skin. Concentrate on those places that rarely feel the touch of lips, such as the back of the neck, the inside of the upper thigh, the small of the back. Cycle the passion with periods of conscious rest, focusing on your breath to help still any distracting thoughts that might arise. In these moments, become aware of both heartbeats bringing you together as one. In this way you can intensify the build toward the ecstatic release.

Understanding the Ego

Remember that when living from your ego the concern is solely for yourself—it's all about your need to be right, to be in control, to be justified in your actions. In the silence of meditation, you will be able to recognize the manipulation of your ego and learn to use it for a greater good. The intention is not to attempt to kill off your ego, but to include it in the process of learning to love unconditionally.

David Richo, in his book *How to Be an Adult in Relationships: The Five Keys to Mindful Loving,* outlines the five fundamental mindsets of ego that interrupt our ability to be here now and that distort reality. The five mindsets—fear, desire, judgment, control, and illusion—should not be viewed as bad. Each of these mental afflictions have a particular energy that can be used for positive mindfulness. The point is not to attempt to rid yourself of these mindsets but to channel their energies to work for, rather than against, you in relationships. In other words:

- *Fear* can be a warning to be more cautious
- *Desire* allows you to open and reach out to others
- *Judgment* fosters viewing a situation with intelligence,
- *Control* is needed to maintain some stability in your everyday life
- *Fantasy* stimulates the imagination and fosters creativity.

When we learn how to befriend these mindsets, we gain useful tools to support our spiritual growth and awakening.

Careful What You Ask For

"It is said that there are only two tragedies in life: not getting what one wants, and getting it."
—Bhante Henepola Gunaratana

One of my students related a story to me about how she had wished to meet a man who would satisfy her description of a perfect partner. Someone suggested that she find a picture in a magazine of someone who represented what she wanted in looks and personality. She found a full-page vodka advertisement featuring a handsome, blond, 30-something man relaxing on a large yacht. In her imagination, he was someone who loved to travel, who sought adventure and excitement, was fun to be around, and had the good looks and physique she fanta-sized about. She taped the ad to her refrigerator door and looked at it every day, visualizing herself with him and dreaming of how perfect they would be together. Eventually she met a man who, in looks and temperament, could have been a twin of the model in the ad. The only problem, she later came to discover, was that he was an alcoholic; coincidentally, his drink of choice was vodka.

As amazing as it may seem, you create your reality by what you program your mind to think. You then take those thoughts, fueled by desire, and manifest them in the world. A desire for perfection gets you in trouble more often than not. Your delusions and attachments make dispelling the fantasy of the perfect mate difficult. Use this next practice to clear away any past picture of what you want in a mate and see what arises for you in this present moment of your life.

Practice

Take a moment to sit quietly and ask yourself what love and intimacy mean to you. Bring into your mind your image of the perfect mate. Visualize what he or she looks like, how the person moves, smiles, speaks with you. Don't judge your choice; rather, let the images arise naturally and spontaneously.

Notice what you like and dislike about the picture you see. Step back and observe your mind as it creates the fantasy of what it wants, pieced together from what it has seen and from what it has been told is the perfect image.

Recognize the illusion you are holding on to in your mind and the feelings of disappointment that arise if you cannot attain your ideal. Now allow your mind to clear as you repeat the first line of the following mantra on the inhale, the second line on the exhale.

Truth Mantra

Breathing in, I release my illusions.
Breathing out, I open to the truth.

As you breathe with the mantra, let yourself go with what is happening. Your thoughts can often surprise you and reveal something you previously might not have admitted. It may be that you don't want to have someone in your life all the time because you are a very independent person; or, thinking you only wanted casual sex and friendship, you find you have been seeking a deeper love all along. This is the nature of the practice—to clear away the smokescreen of thoughts to reveal the truth that lies underneath it all.

Know What You Want and Who You Are

"Know what you want, know what makes you feel good about your Self, know what brings you into harmony with others."

—*I Ching, Book of Changes*

It is up to you to convey to your partner how you want to be loved and to respect how your partner asks to be loved in return. Your lover is not a mind reader—he or she needs to hear from you what turns you on and brings you the greatest pleasure. Acceptance can be both wonderful and challenging at times, always changing with the impermanence that is a constant in our unpredictable lives. It is our attachment to the desire for security and stability that leaves us one step behind the fluctuations of the ever-evolving present moment. How can you expect someone always to be the same when you know yourself to be shifting and changing with each passing second? The constant fluctuations of your thoughts are a good example of the nature of impermanence. Watch how they move from one subject to the next, one fantasy following another, a conversation you had a year ago suddenly switching to a mental list for tomorrow's shopping. Here is proof enough that there is no constant from moment to moment.

By becoming aware of our actions, we can begin to better understand who we are, and this self-knowledge leads to clarity and discernment. When I speak to my friends, I do so with a certain comfort that I will not be judged, that I have already been accepted for who I am. But when I find myself in conversation with a man I am attracted to, I am aware of how my body language changes, awakening a primitive instinct for connection on a different level.

I remember once answering the telephone and hearing the voice of a man I had been seeing. Immediately the tone and quality of my voice changed, my body became soft and sensuous, and I laughed with a deeper sound that spoke of music and wine and two bodies dancing. When I hung up the phone, a friend who had never heard me speak in this way laughed her mocking laugh and said, "Oh, that's your 'speaking-with-a-man' voice. You completely changed your character and became a sultry siren." I blushed with embarrassment, having been caught red-handed as the soft coquette rather than a powerful warrior woman.

I made a mental note of this so that I could observe my behavior when I was once again in this man's presence. I saw then the truth of how I can be when I am swimming in the sea of a desire. There was no judgment to be made, nor criticism, but it allowed me to look deeper at my motivation for wanting to attract this person, and the ways I have used this in other relationships in my past. Knowing this, I was able to see whether I was being honest with myself and with him and to consider whether I was thinking only about what I wanted or whether I was thinking about what was right for him as well.

Practice

In your journal record your observations about your relationship with your spouse, lover, or potential partner. Over time, as you continue making journal entries, you should begin to notice whether you act solely in your own self-interest or whether you also consider what pleases and makes the other person happy. If each of you is thinking of the other's needs first, you are both sure to get what makes you feel good.

Take a few moments to list ...

- What you want from your partner.
- What makes you feel good about yourself.
- What brings you into harmony with those around you.

Then put your journal aside and sit quietly in meditation, observing the thoughts that come up concerning what you have just written. After a few moments, allow your mind to calm, mentally reciting the Harmony mantra with each inhale and exhale.

Harmony Mantra

Breathing in, I embrace my desires.

Breathing out, I open to my partner's need.

128

Embracing your desires is to know what brings you pleasure. Open to your partner's needs, but be sure to let your partner know how you would like him or her to be fully present to yours. Use your breath to help clear away any restrictions preventing you from feeling the pleasurable sensations that arise in your body.

Eliminating the Barriers to Great Sex

"As the river gives itself into the ocean, what is inside me moves inside you."

—Robert Bly

With the awareness of how ego manipulates our actions, can we honestly open ourselves to a healthy and satisfying sex life? First, we should tackle the question of what constitutes great sex. It might mean to feel nurtured and fully loved by another. Or it might be the immediate satisfaction of sexual desire, with love existing separate from the act of intercourse. It's often the case that women define great sex as the former (as feelings of nurturing and love), and men as the latter (as fulfillment of sexual desire, pure and simple). Right away there is tension, and so begins the dance to get what each person wants from the other. If we are so concerned about our own personal needs and desires, can we really come together and experience the ecstasy and bliss that true union can create?

Great sex is the result of your passion to share yourself in the act of lovemaking. If you are ashamed or critical of your body, you will be shy and hesitant to let yourself go completely. Take some time to look at yourself naked in front of a mirror. Better still, put on some music that gets your hips moving and do a striptease for yourself, uncovering your body one limb at a time. Let your eyes take in the strengths and weaknesses that the mirror reflects back to you.

This is the body you were born with. There's no use fighting the truth of what you see, so you might as well accept the reality. You can always imagine what your body might look like after changing your diet and getting more exercise, but in this moment allow loving kindness to fill your heart in gratitude for your body as is—what supports your life here on Earth. Let that love become joy in what you have to share with someone else. If you are big and soft, know that your roundness will be a warm cushion of comfort. It is the consideration and kindness you show to your partner—not what you look like—that makes for great sex.

Nobody is perfectly content with their looks and the shape of their body, regardless of whether they are tall and thin, short and fat, or utterly perfect to your eyes. It is important in this next practice that you observe, without judgment (that is, I hate my thighs, my breasts are perfect, nose is too big, my biceps are buffed, and so on), the images that surface when considering the different parts of your body. Hating what you have takes up valuable mental energy and harms no one but yourself. Loving your body brings confidence and a strong sense of self.

Get in the Zone

Take some time to learn about the pleasure zones of your and your partner's body. For example, few people know that the only organ in the human body made solely for pleasure is the woman's clitoris. All other organs have multiple functions except for this small but powerful pleasure zone. Allow yourself to embrace the sensual delights that are inherent in your body and available for you to experience.

This next practice can help to foster self-acceptance and gratitude for what you have been given in this lifetime.

Practice

Take a moment to sit quietly, with eyes closed, and allow the image of your body to come into your mind. Notice the thoughts and judgments that surface as you look at each part of your body. Begin with your feet, then your legs, working your way up slowly. Become the detached observer, looking without judging, seeing without drawing a conclusion. Your body is an amazing vehicle you drive in this lifetime. Reciting the Body mantra will help to dispel your quest for the perfect physique and allow you to accept what your body for what it is.

Body Mantra

Breathing in, I accept my body in this moment.

Breathing out, I release my inhibitions and open to the pleasure of passion.

Accept your body for all the wildness and passion that it holds, as well as for the service it gives you day to day.

Listening to Each Other

"Deep listening is really being with another. You're in a state of presence where your mind is not cluttered with past judgments or thoughts of the future. You feel no urgency or impatience, and you let go of beliefs and prejudices you may have about the other person."

—Joseph Bailey

Speaking about sex is very difficult for many people. Yet it is this lack of communication between couples about sex that causes most sexual problems.

It is with an emptiness of mind that we come into the presence of another and fully listen to what he or she tells us. Don't let the constant chatter of the mind separate you from the moment and from what your partner is trying to tell you. Don't interrupt and express your feelings first, because it will only put the other on the defensive. This is what the practice of meditation, of learning to quiet the mind and focus on a single point, prepares you for.

Practice

In the beginning it isn't easy to let go of what's in your mind, your opinions, your rehearsed statements, or your conflicted emotions. When you and your partner need to talk, plan a moment when neither of you are rushed and there is time to be together fully. Either sit cross-legged on cushions with your knees touching or in comfortable chairs facing each other. Decide who will begin. It is important that the listening partner not interrupt or formulate a response while the other person is speaking.

When the first speaker is done, switch roles. Go back and forth in this way until you have exhausted the topic and you have reached an understanding. When this is complete, acknowledge that are you finished and agree that you can return for further discussion once you both have had time to think. Agree that neither of you will ever use what is said against each other in any way. When you have both expressed yourselves, take a moment to sit quietly. Hold hands, close your eyes, focus on your breath, and say the Partners mantra silently to yourself with each inhale and exhale.

Partners Mantra

> *Breathing in,* I am complete and at peace.
>
> *Breathing out,* I am open to love.

As the breath quiets, the thoughts in your mind fill the emptiness with this mantra and allow your heart to open to a renewed love for each other. It is important to come away complete with what has passed between you. Take a moment to wrap your arms around each other and stay in this embrace for a few minutes. Let the feelings of forgiveness and loving kindness surface with gratitude for what has been shared and released.

Moving Meditation: Compassionate Sex

It takes practice to let go of what you want and focus on pleasuring your partner. As you give of yourself fully, however, you may find that you experience immense joy and satisfaction that comes with surrendering in this special moment. This moving meditation encourages you to practice loving kindness with your partner. Use this experience to open fully to the joy of doing for someone else, while asking nothing in return. As you move through the motions, recite the mantra silently to yourself. Let the words open your heart and quiet your mind.

Plan some uninterrupted time with your partner, when neither of you have to rush. Unplug the telephones and create a quiet space to be together. Purchase a bottle of body massage oil and prepare the room by lighting candles, burning incense, or warming a relaxing aromatherapy oil, such as lavender or ylang ylang. Play some romantic music to enhance this moment of intimacy.

Begin by massaging your partner's body with soft, gentle strokes, staying present to his or her reactions. Moving your hands gently over the skin, softly ask your partner what he or she would like you to do. Listen with no expectations or agenda.

Allow yourself to flow with the moment, doing what your partner requests. Let go of your own desires and stay mindful that you are here to please this person. Let this be a gift of compassion from your heart to his or hers, for it is in this unconditional giving that you can receive your greatest pleasure.

Love Mantra

Breathing in, I express unconditional love.

Breathing out, I give with compassion and loving kindness.

Use this mantra to help you stay focused on your lover, instead of being distracted by other thoughts. Unconditional love is giving without expectation of receiving anything in return. Compassion and loving kindness are the full embodiment of your heart opening to another.

Guided Meditation: Journey of the Heart

Deep love goes beyond self and commitment with one person. It is an all-encompassing passion that reaches out to the world and gathers everything into its embrace. The meditation practice used to learn compassion and loving kindness traditionally uses the Buddhist chant "May all sentient beings enjoy happiness and the root of happiness." This practice is based on extending love out to yourself, those you love, as well as those people who have harmed or angered you.

Begin by taking your seat in meditation and aligning your mind with the flow of your breath. Recite the following Loving Kindness mantras with the sincere intention of letting love and compassion flow from your heart.

Loving Kindness Mantras

For yourself: May I be filled with joy and happiness in my life.

For a friend or loved one: May [friend's name] life be filled with love and happiness.

For someone you have negative feelings for: May [person's name] know joy and peace in his/her life.

For suffering in the world: May all beings be free from suffering.

For all beings: May all beings enjoy peace, love, and happiness.

Send this loving energy out into the world, knowing that your thoughts have the power to create change and the strength of your love can bring freedom from suffering.

Meditation can change the way you relate to people in a profound way. It transforms you from the inside out by opening your heart and your mind, moving you away from a self-centered existence and into the realm of shared life. It brings you to a place of trust where you can give and receive love on a deeper, more intimate, level. Most of all, it is a sacred gift given to us so that we may end our suffering and the suffering of others. All that is required from you is a commitment to right intention and continuous practice.

Chapter 8

The Peaceful Family

"Bring the family to its proper order and all social relationships will be correctly established."
—I Ching

To create a peaceful family requires patience and tolerance mixed with a good dose of love and generosity. Not necessarily an easy combination when the individuals are your brothers, sisters, and parents. Why is that? We tend to act things out with our siblings that we might not with other people. We also have expectations of them that we don't have of anyone else. Then, when things don't go as expected, enmity can result. There are an endless number of family stories to tell illustrating this point, but you each, no doubt, have your own.

Meditation can make family relations easier to deal with and can help strengthen the family bond. As discussed in previous chapters, a daily meditation practice develops patience, understanding, and opens the heart to love more fully.

Your Family Connection

With nearly 50 percent of marriages ending in divorce, that leaves a lot of children being raised without either a mother or father in the home. It also causes many young people to shy away from marriage because they fear that the marriage will only fall apart in the end. How would you describe your present family or the family you plan to have in the future?

If your idea of family is ...

- A place to live when not working
- A duty you must perform
- A restriction on your freedom
- Impossible to maintain in today's culture

... then you will suffer from the chaos and disruption this way of living can bring you.

If, on the other hand, you view family as an opportunity to ...

- Give and receive love
- Create a warm, inviting environment away from the world
- Raise consciously aware children
- Make a positive contribution to your community
- Practice generosity, integrity, trust, and loyalty

... you will overcome the challenges that family life will bring your way.

The Perfect Family

Baby Boomers can remember growing up with *Leave It to Beaver*'s perfect family. Other generations had *The Brady Bunch, The Simpsons, The Sopranos,* and *The Osbournes*. Is it any wonder that our idea of what a family looks like is often warped and confused. Take a moment to think about how you have been influenced by television and movies in shaping your concept of family. Then describe, in your meditation journal, what you consider to be the perfect family.

It is said that we are born into a family, but not always into our tribe, meaning a group of people we have a common affinity with. Do you ever feel like the stork delivered you to the wrong family? Or, to take a popular fairy tale, are you the "ugly duckling" who's hoping, one day, to see yourself for what you really are—a graceful swan?

We can relate the story of the ugly duckling to our lives as spiritual beings having a human experience. We are already enlightened beings (the Swan), born into a world ruled by our deluded ego self (the duckling) and trapped in a cycle of suffering. We identify ourselves by labels that society imposes and that we accept, (I am a doctor, husband, dentist, teacher). As human beings we struggle to find a semblance of our true Self within the framework of what we have been taught and what we choose to believe. Mistaking our Swan nature for the duckling keeps us cycling our conflicted emotions and mental suffering. Sitting quietly in meditation allows our true nature to bleed through the fabric of our conditioning so that we can recognize our beautiful Swan Self as always having been present. We also see the true nature of those around us, including our family.

The Nuclear Family

Nuclear family   A basic social unit consisting of parents and their dependent children living in one household.

—*Webster's New World College Dictionary,* Fourth Edition

The traditional two-parent home has changed with the times. It is not uncommon to have single-parent (from divorce) families, families with adopted children of a different ethnic heritage, same-sex parents with children, single adults with children, and families of children who have lost their parents to disease. When considering marriage and raising a family, nothing is as we were taught it should be. Thus is the nature of impermanence and change.

Medical intuitive and spiritual teacher Carolyn Myss says that we come into this lifetime having made "sacred contracts" with other souls we will meet in human form. The Dalai Lama reminds us to be kind to others because they may have been your mother in a previous incarnation. Whatever you believe your connection to be with your family, they are individuals who can tax your patience, your tolerance, and your ability to love unconditionally. Parents, in particular, often start families with the expectation that their children will be perfect little gems and grow up to be just the way they want them to be. A meditation practice can help to alleviate some of the suffering caused by holding on to our familial fantasies.

For instance, a wild and independent soul born into a strongly disciplined family will need room to stretch his or her wings rather than be forced to conform. The child who is expected to become a doctor and shows talent and a love for music must be recognized for the child's own strengths rather than the parent's attachment to a vision they have for him or her. As a parent, the practice of meditation can help you to see past your own illusions of your child's future—the future you have so carefully envisioned over the years—the one that can cause you great suffering when the child stands up for himself or herself as an individual and decides to follow his or her own path.

Marlon had a wild, independent spirit. His father was in the military, and both of his parents were devout Catholics. It soon became apparent that Marlon was a round peg trying to fit into a square hole. As hard as he tried, he could not reshape his nature to conform with the restrictions of his parents' beliefs. Over time his round peg began to distort; the shape of his personality became twisted, sanded, and cracked as his parents tried to make him live according to their own ideals. When he became an adult, his life spiraled out of control as he searched for his true identity after a childhood of repression. He always felt that he was in the wrong tribe.

Marlon began a study of meditation when he saw that the spiritual path described by the Buddha is one of going against the stream, against the repression and ignorance aimed at subduing the free spirit. His whole life had been in opposition to his parents and society as a whole. In meditation he was able to let go of his attachment to suffering as an act of rebellion against what everyone else was doing. In doing so, he saw that what he thought was freedom through drugs and alcohol was just a trap of pleasure following pain. In meditation he found that he could get in touch with the truth of how much pain his lifestyle caused him and those he loved. He was able to allow life to unfold in its own way, its own time, and yet know that he could work to change what he saw was wrong in the world. He had come to meditation in terrible pain and found freedom from trying to control the uncontrollable—the mind, the body, and the world.

When Marlon shared his meditation experience with his parents they told him that they found this freedom in their devotion to prayer and the sanctity of the church. They admitted that their faith had been challenged by a lifetime of his wildness, but had always prayed that he would find his way. Marlon realized that his parents had provided him with his greatest challenge of acceptance and understanding. They each had learned that they were on the same spiritual journey, but needed to respect the vehicle chosen to make the trip.

In comprehending our roles in each other's lives, we can bring a deeper understanding to how we play out our lives together.

Families that meditate gain a clear vision of how each individual can be a mirror for the other, while also recognizing that each member of the family is unique in his or her own way and must be honored for that distinction. Holding up the mirror means you are able to support each other's ability to stay present without undo judgment or criticism. As parents you shape your children according to how you were shaped by your parents. You teach your kids what you learned from your parents, good or bad, and you do so based on your attachment to being right. Why? Because as an adult you think you know better—after all, you're the adult, right?

Meditation gives you the clarity to see that, as parents, you have the responsibility of guiding your children to find their place in the world, helping them to understand what their duty in life will be. After they have found it, from your living example, they will know to do it. As my father once told me, "Find what you love to do and do it to the best of your abilities."

Practice

Sit comfortably. Close your eyes and focus your mind on the exhale of your breath. Allow your mind to calm and your thoughts to fade into the background. Now imagine a river moving through a forest of trees. Imagine yourself standing on the bank of that river.

It may be that at this moment your life is in turmoil and so the river is racing by, crashing around boulders in its way. Or it may be a tranquil time for you, and so the water moves with a slow, even flow.

Look upriver and see your family members floating toward you. Knowing your family, you will see who has the big inner tube and a six pack of beer, the one stretched out on his/her back gazing up at the sky undisturbed, the one giving orders, or the one afraid of someone being hurt. They are all in your life stream, and as they draw near to where you stand they call to you to step out into the water and join them.

In your way, whether swimming, floating, or grabbing a piece of wood to hold on to, enter the river and join your family. Visualize each member taking another's hand until you become a human chain moving with the flow of the water. Feel the strength that comes from this bond. Draw from the feeling of support as each rapid or boulder appears before you. Use the Bonding mantra to stay present to your vision.

Bonding Mantra

> *Breathing in,* I am the breath for my family.
>
> *Breathing out,* My family is the breath for me.
>
> *Breathing in,* I am the strength of my family.
>
> *Breathing out,* My family is the strength for me.

Nothing is so powerful as the bond of family love. To go through life knowing there are others out there in the world who care so much about you they will come to your aid on a moment's notice (or you to theirs) gives you one of your deepest levels of connection to others. Before dismissing the dysfunctions of your family as unbearable, make the effort to heal your connection with them, if this is at all possible.

Karma in Family Relationships

According to Buddhist teachings, the law of karma can be carried from one lifetime to the next and can determine the situation you are born into. Often, the most important relationships you have in life are those with your immediate family. These can also be your most challenging, terrifying, supportive, and joyful. It makes sense, then, that your family has probably been a part of your previous incarnations. You and your family have a particular "karma" to complete together in this lifetime.

Not long ago I sat at the bedside of a young man who was dying of cancer. He had showed up in a morning yoga class some two years before, a handsome and robust 27-year-old with his head shaved. After class he told me that he had been battling Hodgkins disease for three years, and that he was on the upswing and would be coming to class more often. Now, two years later, I gazed upon his shrunken form and he spoke of his illness as karma for previous lifetimes. He said that he had an insight during meditation where he saw himself as his uncle who had died a painful death as a young man. He felt that he had been his uncle and reincarnated into the same family to once again die a painful death as a young man. He didn't know how many times he would have to pay for his actions, not knowing what they might have been, but he felt in his heart that this was the path toward freeing himself of any harm he had caused others.

Buddhist monk Ajahn Chah taught how all things are transient, including love and hate. You can both love your children and at times feel hate for them, as if they were bullets fired back into your heart. For parents, your children are your karma, the good ones as well as the bad ones. For children it is the same; your parents are your karma, for good or bad. How you deal with them in your life depends on how your mind works for good or bad. Know that you will experience both love and hate toward them; when times are most difficult and you want to run away from them all, sit and practice this meditation.

Practice

In the midst of your anger, sit in meditation and observe your thoughts. Remember that all things pass, all emotions and thoughts die away to be replaced by others. Nothing is permanent, and what is occurring in your mind will shift and change. Use the Grounding mantra to help move you through the moment, letting the anger arise and pass away without suppressing what you are feeling.

Grounding Mantra

Breathing in, Love is transient.

Breathing out, Hate is transient.

Breathing in, Anger will pass.

Breathing out, Calm will come.

Breathing in, All thoughts arise.

Breathing out, All thoughts fall away.

When you experience anger and negative thoughts, the feelings come from your mind. Nobody put those feelings there but yourself, and no one but you can let them go. When your mind is agitated and you look to blame someone else, turn your gaze within and see that the cause lies there and not outside of you. To create peace between yourself and others, you must first look within and correct your mind's afflictions.

Creating Peace Within the Family

"It's painful to face how we harm others, and it takes a while. It's a journey that happens because of our commitment to gentleness and honesty, our commitment to staying awake, to being mindful."

—Pema Chodron

What better way to practice compassion and loving kindness than with your family members. In every family there's someone who pushes your buttons—the alcoholic brother, the sister who "borrows" your things and never returns them, the niece or nephew on drugs, the father who fools around, the suffering mother, Mom or Dad's favorite child. Rather than see how much distance you can put between yourself and this person, give thanks that you have someone to teach you life's greatest lessons: patience, tolerance, compassion, and loving kindness.

Don't think for a moment that this will be easy just because you're related to each other. In some ways it will be more difficult because of the pattern that was established over a long period of time. It's all that water under the bridge that tends to flood the forgiveness channels.

Calling home one winter to inquire about my mother's failing health, my sister lashed out at me, angry that I was so far away during this family crisis. I could feel my own anger rise in retaliation. Here was familiar territory, and I tensed for the coming battle. In the instant that my angry response rose to the surface of my consciousness, it instantly dissolved. In that space I was able to see her pain and fear masquerading as anger.

I responded by calmly asking her how she was handling everything, and, given no fuel to stoke her anger, she began to calm down. In recognizing her pain as my own, I was able to shift the energy from anger to compassion, which literally means "suffering with." My meditation practice enabled me to step past my ego reaction and see what was happening in the moment, free of our past history. The next morning she e-mailed me to apologize for her outburst. In the space I had given her, she had immediately recognized how superfluous her anger was and had the strength of character to correct it.

Healing Old Wounds and Addictions

Simon was the oldest in a family of three boys and two girls. He worked for a baseball team as a talent scout and had access to tickets for important games. This particular year his team won the playoffs and was going to the World Series. His sister asked him to get tickets for her husband and other siblings. He gladly agreed and acquired the tickets for the whole family to go. Everyone was thrilled. Their favorite team was to play, and elaborate plans were made for transportation and lodging out of town.

A few days before the big game, an important client offered Simon several thousand dollars for the tickets. Simon, who needed the extra money to help pay his family's bills, accepted the offer without consulting the rest of the family. He assumed that everyone would understand; just in case they didn't, however, he had his wife break the news. Three years later, the families are still not speaking to each other.

Simon thought that his family would be happy for his windfall. An opportunity had presented itself when he needed money, and he grabbed it. What was wrong with that? Simon's fear of not having enough ran smack into his greed when confronted with abundance. His separation from others allowed him to give no thought to their feelings. Because they were family, he figured they would get over their disappointment.

The family, on the other hand, was furious that their plans were crushed. Attached to having free tickets for the World Series, their joy and happiness quickly turned to pain. All their plans could move forward only if they now paid an exorbitant amount of money for new tickets. Calling Simon, they asked whether they could share in the monies gained from the sale? Simon saw no reason to share the spoils because they had nothing to do with the transaction. His attachment to the money was too great to let go. The family battle became ugly, with anger and hatred building with each day.

When Simon's wife told me the story, I wondered whether he would have sold the tickets if they had been promised to business associates? "Probably not," she said, "his fear of losing his livelihood was stronger than upsetting his family." He never considered that his family would cut him off for selling those tickets.

If each individual involved in this story practiced meditation, the scenario might have played out differently. Aware of their attachment to how they wanted things to turn out, the family members could have more easily released the anger and resentment and reacted to Simon's financial hardship with compassion and support. In Simon's case, practicing meditation would have made him conscious of the importance of his family connection, and he would have gone to them when the offer to sell the tickets came up. When we separate ourselves from others, we act out of our attachments to desire. When there is not "I" or "mine" tied to the situation, there is a letting go. What you see is how the attachments have hold of you as much as you have hold of them.

Having a consistent meditation practice helps you to let go of your attachment to the mental afflictions of anger, jealousy, hatred, and pride. It guides you toward healing old wounds with estranged siblings and parents.

Your practice of meditation may not solve your family's dysfunctions, but it will provide you with a new way to deal with old wounds and issues. Consider the sibling or parent who is trapped in the disease of alcoholism. You and the other family members have tried everything—from pleading, arguing, intervention, and isolation—and nothing has worked. You watch as this person spirals downward to the bottom of life, unable to let go of his or her addiction; and you are unable to let go of what you want for this person.

Here is a great challenge for you. Silently thank this person for this opportunity and set about opening your heart rather than closing down in judgment and anger. Read everything you can about the disease, attend meetings of Alcoholics Anonymous to get support from others in this same situation. And in your meditation, practice Tonglon, the act of taking on the pain of your family member and transforming it to love and happiness.

Practice

Sitting in meditation, bring your focus to your breath and allow your mind to calm. Let the images of your family members come into your mind one at a time. Step back and watch your reactions, judgments, and criticisms. Notice any emotions that come up and let them dissolve, as if the light you shine is a laser of compassion and understanding. You know all their faults and misdeeds. You probably remember childhood fights or abuse and continue to hold on to those memories. In this moment, allow your perspective to change and see them without past or future. This will be very hard to do, so go slowly. Stop if it becomes too much and write down any insights you have in your meditation journal.

In your meditation, see their fear of living life, their anger for what they could not achieve, the suffering caused by layer upon layer of attachment to desires impossible to reach. With each inhale, take in their pain; with each exhale, breathe out and smile. Recite the Compassion mantra to help keep you focused on opening your heart with loving kindness and to keep the past away.

If you or a member of your extended family suffers from an addiction, this can be a powerful, albeit extremely difficult, meditation to practice.

Compassion Mantra

Breathing in, I transform pain into love.

Breathing out, I wish happiness for [say the person's name here].

This may be all you can do at first. In the family, many times their pain is your pain. You were there and saw the suffering, experienced it yourself, and now your siblings or parents are the mirror for your own emotional stew pot. In this practice you can come very close to your connection to all things, beginning with those whose blood you share. Eventually, this brings you to seeing your connection to the African mother dying of AIDS; she is your family member dying. The homeless person who has lost everything in his pursuit of death in the bottle; he, too, is your brother, your sister, your father, or mother. In reality, he is you.

The Spiritual Life of the Householder

"The sacrifices of a family are like those of any demanding monastery, offering exactly the same training in renunciation, patience, steadiness, and generosity."

—Jack Kornfield

In the Pali Canon, the Buddha is quoted as saying "The household life is a dusty path full of hindrances, while the ascetic life is like the open sky. It is not easy for a man who lives at home to practice the holy life in all its fullness, in all its purity, in all its bright perfection." Even Jesus Christ spoke to his followers to "go sell what you possess and give to the poor ... and come follow me." Is it possible to have a deep spiritual life as a householder, or must you renounce the world—and the family life—to attain liberation?

In a culture that has come to embrace all traditions, even so far as calling itself a "melting pot" of humanity, it is no surprise that there is a new democratization of spirituality emerging in America. Spirituality has shifted from the extreme of living life in a cave to having a family life with job, children, and mindful sex. It has emerged as a movement to marry the sacred with the secular, and at the core lies the practice of meditation.

"... when we speak about spiritual practice, like meditation, for example, we use the word 'practice' because it's practice for living," says Elizabeth Lesser, author of *The New American Spirituality*. In other words, practicing meditation prepares you for dealing with a hysterical child, a demanding boss, a mean-spirited co-worker, an inconsiderate spouse, all those situations that come up in life and demand your response.

Of course, you need to take time away from the world to go deeper into your practice, but the point is that you use your life as your practice, connecting all the dots, which lead you to communion with God. True spirituality is not just about attending church on Sunday and then spending the rest of the week fighting with your family, cheating your competition at work, and then stopping off for a lap dance on the way home. It is difficult and arduous work, and it takes a focused mind to stay the course in our overstimulated culture.

As a householder, you will face many distractions in your spiritual quest. You need to earn a living, spend time with your family and provide for their material comforts, and find time to meditate.

The purpose of meditation is to free the mind from attachment. As a householder, you must be willing to completely give up your attachment to the world of ambition, envy, romance, lust for power, greed, hatred and the many other temptations you encounter in life. The ascetic can enter a monastery and is taken out of the distractive world. In the workplace, in the household, and in your interaction with strangers you are consistently challenged to stay true to the principals of right conduct and purity of mind. If you are going to live in the world as a householder, you don't have to struggle financially and live a poor but simple life. Do the work you love to do, but be of service to others as well. Use the money that you make to provide for yourself and your family and to benefit others in the world. Sharing the bounty you have is a lesson in letting go, of practicing loving kindness and generosity. Without this letting go, your practice is of the basic kind and in the end may only serve to feed your ego.

The Family at Play

> "To play with it is therefore not a duty but a joy, and he who does not see it as a joy can neither do it nor understand it."
> —Allan Watts

What if we finally understand that we are here to play with each other joyfully rather than suffer bitterly over inconsequential actions? Philosopher and theologian Allan Watts speaks about how we take ourselves too seriously in our human role on Earth. Children approach life as play, but as adults we forget about the fun and make a religion of the game. We begin to identify with the part or position we are playing, attach ourselves so strongly to the image that we fear losing it. Instead of playing our part freely and joyously, we let the part play us.

To see how this might work in your family, consider how each member identifies with his or her various roles:

- The eldest
- The intellectual
- The baby of the family
- The only child
- The rebel or the black sheep
- The disciplinarian
- The loving parent

Each of these roles comes with a preordained behavior and expectations. Here is that veil of illusion again. This is because we are always trying to measure the infinite. Spiritual teacher and author Deepak Chopra describes how, "Our whole notion of reality has actually been topsy-turvy. Instead of God being a vast imaginary projection, he turns out to be the only thing that is real, and the whole universe, despite its immensity and solidity, is a projection of God's nature." What we take to be real is only Divine Spirit, God, at play. We are literally at "play in the fields of the Lord." This same wisdom teaches that enlightenment is knowing that life is play; we suffer because we take seriously what the gods made for fun. A family united in love and play creates a strength that not only supports the individual members, but also society as a whole.

From my own experience of being raised in a large family, the crucial ingredient to getting along with each other was our collective sense of humor. The ability to laugh through the good and bad times and see the absurdity in our behavior turned many an argument into a festival of humor. The spiritual teacher Osho reminds us that the first thing we should do upon waking is to laugh. This will set the tone for the whole day. When you wake up laughing, you will soon begin to feel how absurd life is, how seriously we take our pain, our disappointments, and our role in life.

As for the family and married life, research has shown that there are greater benefits to being married and having a family than to being single, divorced, or widowed. Married couples ...

- Live longer.
- Drink, smoke, and do drugs less.
- Experience fewer illnesses and disease.
- Have lower rates of suicide.
- Have lower rates of alcoholism.
- Suffer less from depression.
- Are more financially secure.
- Experience higher emotional and sexual satisfaction.

These statistics can be enhanced with the practice of meditation. Parents often remark on how much love and peace surfaced after they began to meditate with their children. Understanding difficult situations is easier, and getting over a conflict happens much more quickly. Children who have been raised in a loving, stable family are more likely to be successful in most all areas of their lives. They are also more willing to marry and raise their children in the same ways, passing on the principles of honesty, integrity, love, and support that they learned from their parents.

Keeping in mind that meditation is about living fully in the moment, staying present to what is happening as it occurs, then your whole life is your practice.

Moving Meditation: Bringing Your Family Together

Because each family is different, I offer you six meditations you can do together. Choose one that seems best-suited to you and your family, or try them all, one at a time. Allow each member to bring his or her own unique contribution to the practice and, most of all enjoy, the process:

- Plan a special time to come together and talk about your day. At first this may feel awkward, especially if you are not used to discussing things together. Have no expectations of anyone, and if someone chooses not to participate let the silence rest easy between you all.

- Laugh together each day, whether you feel like it or not. Begin by having a "who can laugh the loudest" contest or share a joke you heard to get the laughter started. One exercise you can try is for everyone to lay down on their backs, resting their head on another person's stomach. As one person begins to laugh, it becomes like a domino effect, with everyone soon laughing along.

- Sing together. This can be while doing chores around the house, preparing a meal, or hanging out in the living room. Make up the song using your own words. Have one person begin a sentence and another person end it. Use an old tune, try it rap style. It may sound funny, absurd, or brilliant—just let it flow.

- At least once or twice a week cook a healthful meal together. Plan what you will make from scratch, shop together for the ingredients, and then work together in the kitchen while preparing the food. This is a good time to sing, talk about the day, your plans for vacation, and what's going on in your lives.

- Have dinner together each night. Bring the family together with gratitude for the bounty. Eat mindfully, staying present to the flavors and the satisfaction that comes with being nurtured by delicious food.

- Wake up a few minutes early and sit in meditation together. Take 5 or 10 minutes to center and focus your minds in preparation for the day.

Use the Family mantra before your meals, discussions, or meditation to establish your intentions with a clear understanding as to why you are coming together.

Family Mantra

Breathing in, I accept you for who you are.
Breathing out, I allow love and compassion to flow between us.
Breathing in, I open my heart
Breathing out, I listen with my whole being.

Guided Meditation: Stilling the Mind Together

At what age do you teach your children to meditate with you? As soon as they understand your explanations and instructions, they can begin to sit with you. In this meditation, bring your family together and sit on cushions in a circle on the floor or on straight-backed chairs.

Have everyone rest their hands on their knees, with their spines lifted and all tension in the shoulders and jaw released. Have everyone close their eyes and focus on their own breath, observing the natural flow that occurs spontaneously.

Allow for five minutes to pass and then ring a small bell or gently strike the edge of a glass to bring them back to attention. Share with each other what came up for them while in meditation and what they noticed about their breath.

Practice this together with your loved ones on a regular basis. Have each one recite the Focus mantra silently to himself or herself while observing his or her own inhale and exhale of breath.

Focus Mantra

Breathing in, I calm my mind.

Breathing out, I focus with love.

Over time this practice can extend longer. You may want to learn a few sacred chants to do together, because their purpose is to cleanse and focus the mind. If one member chooses just to sit quietly, the other members should respect that person's need for stillness. This time together should be spent without expectations or judgment and should be shared with a bond of consideration and love.

Chapter 9

Mindful Work

"The things we do for love are rarely the things we do for money."
—Marcia Menter

As a young child, you had probably already started thinking about what you wanted to "be" when you grew up. You probably discovered things about yourself—your likes and dislikes, talents and skills—that led you to dream of certain types of jobs. Teacher, acrobat, firefighter, painter, veterinarian, astronaut, sailor, goalie—children's dreams for themselves are often big and bold, ripe with possibility.

Unfortunately, all too many kids have their visions dashed before they ever have a chance to take root. Instead of pursuing their own dreams, they end up living other people's dreams. How many boys and girls grew up to be doctors when they really wanted to play the drums, or flight attendants when they really wanted to pilot the plane?

Doing Work You Love

People often fail in their careers because they have been trying to live out someone else's idea of what a life's work should be. They go through the day feeling miserable in their job, unable to give 100 percent to the work and their co-workers, seeing their future mapped out before them in one long agonizing stretch of time. Joseph Campbell once said that if you can see your life laid out for you, then you know it's not your life.

Your meditation practice can help you ...

- Find your true vocation.
- Work with acceptance in your present job.
- Understand the impact of the work you are doing.
- Ease conflict with co-workers.
- Deal with your negative emotions.
- Accept your place in the world.

Wouldn't it be wonderful if you could wake up each morning anticipating the possibilities to come, rather than dreading the predictable? The struggles, sufferings, and disappointments you experience are easier to deal with when you are engaged in work that you love. Combined with the insights and mindfulness that meditation teaches you, work becomes challenging play as you learn to dance with your Divine Self, and thus contribute to both your inner spiritual journey and the external world you live in.

We are fortunate to live in a culture in which we are free to choose a means of providing for ourselves and our families. Seek work that calls to you in some heartfelt way.

Feeling Trapped

Eduardo had a college degree in romantic poetry, but to support himself he worked as a waiter in a restaurant. He hated the hours, the exhausting work, the smell of food on his clothes, and the people constantly demanding something from him. His earnings from his poetry weren't enough to live on, though, so he stayed with the job, and as time went by, his anger and frustration increasingly seeped into his poems.

In an attempt to ease his stress and mental anguish, he began practicing meditation. As he let go of his hatred for his job, he noticed how the images that came up were the very things he needed to be writing about. The characters he dealt with each day, the smells, sounds, and dialogue of his customers were all unsung poems waiting to be brought to life. He realized that he was wasting an opportunity to gather valuable information, images, and insight into the nature of people and their culture. With this understanding, he began to write poems more powerful than he ever imagined that he could.

If you are engaged in a job that is a cause of misery, consider what the Buddha advised his followers: "Believe nothing merely because you have been told it, or because it is traditional, or because you yourself imagined it. But whatever way, by thorough examination, you find to be one [path] leading to good and happiness for all creatures, that path follow like the moon the path of the stars." In other words, follow your own heart, listen to the inner voice that tells you what will make you happy. Follow the path of integrity, goodness, and purity of mind, but most of all be true to yourself.

Naturally you will experience fear as you begin to follow your intuition and pursue your dreams. But what if Michelangelo resisted his desire to be an artist because his father insisted he become a merchant, or Wordsworth put down his pen never to write a poem for fear of not having money to support his family? It takes courage and great strength to take a stand for what you believe in and to have confidence that you will succeed in your endeavors.

Right Livelihood

Right livelihood is one of the eight noble paths—the attitudes and actions the Buddha laid out as forming the core of a spiritual practice.

Right livelihood means that one must work in an occupation that benefits others and harms no one.

Yes, well, easier said than done for many people. When people are forced to work in conditions that are harmful to their health or to the environment because they need that paycheck, what is the alternative? The Dalai Lama, when asked a similar question, responded that "It may be necessary to fight against injustice outwardly, but at the same time we have to cope inwardly, with ways to train our minds to remain calm and not develop frustration, hatred, or despair. That's the only solution." Employing what he calls "analytical meditation," the Dalai Lama instructs us to reflect deeply and at length on alternative ways of viewing our situations. Then we can take the appropriate action.

We tend to lock ourselves into thinking that there is only one way, and even if that way is destroying our health, we think we must stay with the job and do nothing. Take, for example, farm workers subjected to pesticide poisoning, or the carcinogenic chemicals that workers inhale in a number of industry jobs. We find ourselves in a paradox: Without employment we cannot pay the bills; without our health, we cannot work. This lesson extends well beyond an individual's personal job concerns to a nation that needs to take compassionate action toward providing safe working conditions for all its citizens and for the environment in which we all live.

Yaqui sorcerer Don Juan spoke of following a path with heart:

Any path is only a path, and there is no affront, to oneself or to others, in dropping it if that is what your heart tells you ...

Look at every path closely and deliberately. Try it as many times as you think necessary. Then ask yourself and yourself alone one question: Does this path have a heart?

If the path does, it is good. If not, it is of no use.

The job you do each day, the career you embark upon for the next stage of your life, the calling you answer to fulfill your destiny are all paths you follow to learn your lessons as a spiritual being. Using what you have come to know about yourself from the quiet observance of your thoughts, consider whether the work you do has a heart big enough to bring you joy and happiness, large enough to teach you how to become more compassionate and loving, and strong enough to support your day-to-day struggles in the workplace.

Find Pleasure in What You Do

"Meditation is your birthright! It is there, waiting for you to relax a little so it can sing a song, become a dance."

—Osho

Ten years ago I found myself at a crossroads in life and decided to take a sabbatical from work. In some professions this is encouraged and supported by the employer, and everyone who can should take advantage of it. In my case, I found that I was exhausted from years of working without a respite and that my work no longer brought me the joy it once did. As I stood looking out at my future, I saw how I was neglecting the present. So I stopped worrying about what the future held and began to play.

Each morning I awoke happy just to do my yoga and meditate, prepare some food, read books, and work to shut down the air-polluting garbage incinerator in our county. (I couldn't keep completely still!)

I knew that I wanted to benefit my community and, hopefully, the world in some way. I also knew that my work would be my play, that each day I would rise to a sense of joy that I loved spending my time serving the Divinity of God. Walking in the forest one afternoon, I understood that this sabbatical had been what I needed to find a new direction for my life, one that came from my meditation and yoga practice, one that would energize rather than exhaust me—but most of all, a life filled with play and laughter.

Play creates fun and profit. It opens up channels of creativity and increases satisfaction in our work lives. *Fortune* magazine research shows that motivated employees are up to 127 percent more productive in highly complex jobs.

All work and no play makes for dull employees. It has been shown that the quality of work suffers without the balance of play and relaxation. A workaholic is as much addicted/attached to work as an alcoholic is to alcohol. We delude ourselves into thinking that by filling our time with work we will come to find a sense of completeness. Best let that one go.

Play allows for thoughts to germinate. Stepping away from the work grind to play and meditate gives the mind a rest, so that it can be more productive and efficient.

We all want to be happy, and yet we set ourselves up to suffer and struggle with our attachment to things that cannot bring us happiness. The Four Noble Truths instruct us in the cause of suffering and how to bring it to an end. The Buddha intended them to give structure to your meditation practice, indeed, to your life in general. Use them as a guide-line in finding balance in your workplace and surrender to the play inherent in all situations.

Practice

Take a moment in your meditation to focus on the work that you do for a living. Is it something you look forward to doing each day? What do you like about the work, your co-workers, your boss, the building you work in? Write these thoughts in your meditation journal and then come back to the breath.

If your job is causing you to be miserable, affecting your life in a negative way, consider doing something to change your present situation. In your journal, make a list of subjects that interest you, such as ...

- Teaching.
- Gardening.
- Antiques.
- Selling.

With an open mind and a belief that all things are possible, take the time to research what is involved in doing some of the jobs you dream of doing. Don't forget to look into ...

- Workload.
- Hours per week.
- Pay scale.
- Insurance and vacation benefits.
- Freedom of expression.
- Opportunity for advancement.

Consider how each job fits with your ...

- Personality.
- Financial needs.
- Abilities.
- Values.

Narrow your list down to a handful of choices and consider what you will need to qualify for each job that remains on your list. You may need to go back to school part time, apprentice to a master teacher, or study the subject on your own time. The Internet has any number of courses available for students willing to change their lives.

When you feel deflated and lose your sense of possibility, recite the Transformation mantra to remind you of where your focus should be aimed.

Transformation Mantra

Breathing in, My thoughts create my life.

Breathing out, All things are possible.

There is always an alternative to any situation. It takes honest reflection and focus to find what calls to your heart. When unsure of your interests, look around your home and see what your surroundings say about you. Let your environment and the items you surround yourself with give you clues as to what path you should follow. Make your decision and take action.

Improving Relationships with Co-Workers

"To be attached to one's own happiness is a barrier to the true and perfect path. To cherish others is the source of every admirable quality known."

—Tsongkhapa

Monica hated going in to work each morning. It wasn't her job that was the problem, she liked the work and responsibility, but she couldn't stand her co-workers, and it was making her life a living hell. The office atmosphere was filled with competitive back-stabbing and ugly gossip. She was trying to live a moral life and practice compassion and kindness, but Monica found she was way over her head in this wasp nest.

Monica's meditation practice had taught her a great deal over the years about her interconnectedness to all beings. At home on the cushion, she could relax and let the anger drop away, allowing her thoughts to dissolve in the light of awareness, bringing her peace and calm. She told herself that she had a loving relationship with her husband and kids, she had girlfriends who supported her emotionally, and a community that appreciated the work she did as a volunteer. And yet, as soon as she stepped into the office, all that was forgotten in the battle to survive the day.

She spoke to her meditation teacher about the situation, and he advised her to single out the one co-worker who led the others by being competitive and inconsiderate. Rather than react to this person's anger, her teacher suggested that she observe how it hides his fears of not being good enough, of losing his job, of being overshadowed by the others. This individual's personality was so strong that everyone in the office had been influenced by him and followed his lead. Her teacher suggested that Monica reach deep into her heart and make the first move to approach this person with warmth and understanding instead of avoidance and fear.

Monica took her teacher's suggestion to the meditation cushion and watched her own resistance and fear emerge at the prospect of confronting her co-worker, John, with kindness. She was sure he would find a way to turn her efforts against her and view her as weak. Then she realized that this was the purpose of meditation, to move past the fear in order to express her inherent goodness. She knew that John was in deep emotional pain, so, each time he confronted her she gave him a warm smile and let his anger wash right over her.

Pretty soon the other people in the office noticed that Monica was not being affected by John's bullying ways, and they began to relax and lighten up toward him. As Monica watched in amazement, the whole atmosphere in the office began to shift for the better. As they each stopped reacting in fear to John's anger, he had no one to feed his drama and became easier to deal with. One day he asked Monica how she could maintain her calm in the face of his anger and she told him about meditation. Not long afterward, he took a course in Transcendental Meditation and eventually credited Monica for having changed his life.

It only takes one person in a group to influence the energy of that group, for good or bad. Bring the light into each conversation, treat the others according to their inherent Divine Nature, and observe what happens.

Recognize Your Connections with Your Colleagues

In the workplace, we are dependent on each other to get the work done and must support each other in doing so. No one person can do it all, and our livelihood depends on others. It doesn't mean you have to like or hang out with each other, but creating a work environment in which everyone gets along and supports the work being done is vital.

In our tendency to see ourselves as separate from others, we overlook the struggles and mental sufferings of our co-workers. In a hostile environment, more than likely your co-workers' outbursts have nothing at all to do with you, and are instead related to what is going on in their lives away from work. In your meditation, take a look at the people you work with and consider ...

- How each person is unique and different.
- Whether they are happy with their job.
- Whether fear is driving their anger.
- What is happening in their home life.

Finally, remember that they are spiritual beings, just like you.

Pema Chodron writes about how we blame others based on our concepts of what is right or wrong. This erects a barrier that keeps us from communicating genuinely with others and not confronting our own culpability. We do this with our closest friends and family, with our government, with all kinds of things that we don't like about our associates or our society. Chodron says that blaming others is a very common, ancient, well-perfected device for trying to feel better. We are afraid to step forward and take responsibility for fear of feeling unstable and vulnerable. Blaming is a way to protect our hearts—what is soft and open and tender. Rather than own that pain, we scramble to find some comfortable ground.

If you are embroiled in an antagonistic relationship with a co-worker, make sure you take an honest look at how you are contributing to the conflict. The spiritual journey is not meant to be without bumps and mountains to climb. When difficulties present themselves, whether in the form of a co-worker, a boss, your spouse, or the barking dog next door, they are all opportunities to put into practice what we awaken to on the meditation cushion. Notice what happens when you actually give thanks for the challenge and open your heart to compassion, generosity, patience, tolerance, and loving kindness.

Consideration for Others

Just because you practice meditation doesn't mean that you won't experience conflict, anger, or resentment in your work. On the contrary, conflict, anger, and resentment are the reality of human nature. It is how the mind handles these negative emotions that separates those who meditate from those who don't meditate. Meditation helps you to break the cycle of your mental afflictions and surrender your attachment to being controlled by your emotions.

For instance, when confronted with feelings of jealousy for someone's promotion when you deserve the promotion, the practice can keep you centered on the cause of your suffering. In your meditation, consider the work you have done and truthfully consider whether the other person deserved to be promoted over you. Also ask yourself what the new job might have cost you. Perhaps it would entail longer work hours that would keep you from your family, or responsibilities you don't really want to take on.

On the other hand, it may be that in your heart you know you are perfect for that job, and your disappointment is overwhelming your enjoyment of going to work. In this case, broaden your perspective, and see how your attachment to wanting the job so badly is causing your suffering. Ask yourself whether you have enough money to pay the bills and support your family. In a world where many people have lost their jobs, or have no possibility of working, think about how lucky you are to have your needs met.

Getting beyond your negative feelings requires self-reflection. It might help to know that in a study concerning people's satisfaction with their jobs, Robert Rice, Ph.D., reported finding that individuals with more "important" jobs are not any happier than those below them on the pay scale. In other words, your boss must deal with his or her attachments, struggles, and disappointments just as you must deal with yours.

Allowing yourself to feel compassion for someone means anyone, not just the poor and downtrodden. When we look to the rich and famous, what we tend to see is how great their lives appear; however, life has a way of balancing out the positive and negative for everyone.

Which brings me to your relationship with your boss. Or maybe you're the boss. In that case, how do you treat your employees?

Dealing With the Boss from Hell

Melanie practices meditation and yoga and works consciously to live a good, pure life. She is a schoolteacher and is known to give 100 percent of herself to her work. In her school, the principal is a political player who deals with the teachers and the higher administration as if he were running for office. Big smiles, lots of handshakes, and promises that this and that would be done—by the end of the day, however, very little is ever accomplished. Then there is the assistant principal, who is basically a very unhappy woman and takes it out on anyone who dares to stand out and excel in his or her job.

In her first year as a teacher in the school district, word got back to other teachers and the administration that Ms. Melanie's class was the students' favorite. Melanie was unprepared for the backlash that came from doing a good job. The assistant principal singled her out and systematically set about destroying Melanie's reputation, all the while acting as if she were a concerned friend.

Other teachers avoided Melanie in the lounge and stopped cooperating with lesson plans that might include her. No one would tell Melanie what was going on. She would get up an hour early each morning to sit and meditate. She told me that it helped her to stay focused on being there for the children and it was what saved her sanity in the face of this adversity.

Finally, she was called into the principal's office and accused of drinking alcohol on the job. The assistant principal was there to reveal her concern with a sad smile on her face. Melanie was stunned. Looking around the room, she let them know that she didn't even drink alcohol, never touched it. The principal looked at his assistant, whose turn it was to look stunned. The assistant principal hadn't done her homework before pointing an accusing finger and ended up being transferred to another school, only this time as the principal.

Melanie was able to use her meditation practice to support her through a very difficult time. Aware of the impermanence of everything in life, she knew that what was happening would pass and everything would be revealed. With that understanding, she was able to go about her job teaching the children without being distracted by the politics around her. After having been exonerated, many of the teachers came to say how sorry they were to have said or done nothing in her defense out of their own fear of the assistant principal. They also remarked on how inspired they were by Melanie's integrity and conduct over those months.

Practice

It's been a long day and you return home tired and ready to put your feet up and read the paper. As soon as you walk in the door, your partner begins a long litany of what needs to be done around the house, how the kids have been driving him/her crazy, and that your boss called to say he needs the report on his desk by tomorrow morning. Suddenly you are angry with everyone; your spouse, boss, and your kids make up the sum total of your fury and you are tempted to let fly with a few choice words and go stay in a hotel for the night. Your mind is racing with questions—*Why do I have to do all the work? Why can't they see that I'm stressed to the max? Why can't they see me, me, me …?*

Instead of lashing out at someone or something, steady your mind by breathing into your anger and watching it dissipate in the gaze of mindfulness. If necessary excuse yourself from the situation and take a moment to sit quietly, letting the emotions melt away to be replaced with a calm and peaceful state of mind.

In this space of emptiness, you can see how tired and stressed your partner is from his or her day, how your children have been under pressure from school and keeping face with their friends, and how the boss is stuck with having to present your report to the owner of the company. All the way up the chain of events, there is the same disturbance of mind, and it has come to rest at your feet. Bring your focus back to your breath, repeating the Anger mantra to yourself as you inhale and again as you exhale.

Anger Mantra

Breathing in, I receive the anger of others.

Breathing out, I calm my mind.

Meditation on the Job

"Those who know others are intelligent; those who know themselves are truly wise. Those who master others are strong; those who master themselves have true power."

—Lao-Tzu

Each morning, in workplaces all over the country, people turn off the ringers on their telephone, close their eyes, and meditate. When they finish meditating, they start their workday alert, creative, energized, and organized. Before leaving for home, those same people once again close the door to the office, turn off the telephone ringer, and meditate. This enables them to wind down from the tension of the day, leaving them completely refreshed and alert for the evening commute and still energized to exercise or be involved in family activities upon arriving home.

Making time each day for meditation is much more profound than simply a physiological way of relaxing. It's a way of becoming whole, of experiencing our deep inner connectedness as human beings. This experience can give a far greater capacity than health and healing. It can open the workplace to ...

- Greater creativity and improved productivity.
- Improved relations among co-workers.
- Improved job satisfaction of employees.
- A friendlier, less-stressed work environment.
- Reduced absenteeism.
- Reduced drug and alcohol abuse.

Employees who are awake, aware, and mindful of what is happening around them in each moment are not only more productive, they also make fewer mistakes, are more efficient, and help create a pleasant work environment.

Handling Time Constraints and Stress

Monday morning used to be the signal that it was time to return to work, after a relaxing weekend of activities with the family and friends. However, more and more people are taking their work home with them to keep up with the ever-increasing load and to prove that they are worth keeping through the next "downsizing." Despite the technology that was developed to make the office less stressful (or maybe because of it?), people are pushed to accomplish much more than they did in the past in the same amount of time. Added to this is the stress of raising a family and finding time to exercise and stay healthy.

Meditation has been shown to improve brain function in practitioners. Research has shown that your oxygen consumption and metabolic rate can decrease as much as 16 percent within 10 minutes of beginning meditation. As you race to keep up with the increasingly fast-paced, digital world, meditation can teach you how to remain calm amid chaos and resist the negative pressure that pushes you to do more and more, faster and faster. It affects your whole life in such a positive way that your family and colleagues will start noticing that you are a happier, more pleasant person to be around. You will find work less stressful and more satisfying. With mindfulness and awareness, you will be able to achieve more in less time in both your work and play because you can filter out extraneous distractions.

Meditation is a priceless gift you can give to yourself to balance a hectic work schedule. It's a gift any company can give to their employees—one that will open the door to a new and vibrant well-being that makes people more calm, resilient, and emotionally strong.

As a matter of fact, many companies encourage their employees to take time each day to meditate. They discovered that meditation …

- **Improved job performance.** For instance, top executives with high levels of responsibility who meditate showed a greater increase in performance than those who didn't meditate and worked at less-responsible levels.

- **Increased speed in problem solving.** Meditation will increase clarity and efficiency in your daily routine while improving your ability to unconsciously process and organize your thoughts.

- **Improved relations with co-workers.** Meditation brings about harmonious interactions within organizations.

- **Enhanced job performance and job satisfaction.** Employees practicing meditation for an average of 11 months showed significant work improvement.

Mindful Planning

Planning your day with mindfulness can include making sure you get to work on time in the morning as well as complete your assignments on time. Repeatedly putting things off until tomorrow is a clear sign that you're not staying present to what needs to be done today. This can result in missed opportunities and mediocre work as you rush to catch up with your work. However, procrastination should be distinguished from intuitive waiting. Although they may appear to be the same thing, intuitive waiting is simply knowing when a little more time is needed to complete what could be a great project as opposed to a mediocre one. Time pressures often have us handing in the mediocre, because it's not always possible to do otherwise. Or is it?

For years I mistook as procrastination my need to think through what I was doing. As I came to know myself better, through my meditation practice, I saw how I would put things together in my head, do my research, make notes, chew on it for awhile, and then put it all together. That was how I worked best, and I got it all done with high marks. I found that there is time for everything if I plan it out properly. I've come to understand how easy life can flow if we would only get out of the way and stop blocking it.

Plan, Then Act

Proper planning and mindful awareness are as important for your meditation or yoga practice as they are for other areas of your life. When students come to me and say that they would like to move their yoga practice to the next level, I ask them if they are trying to rush into something they are not prepared for and should consult their body first. The mind/ego might know where it wants to go, but the body is still trying to stretch out hamstrings taut from 10 years of running. I tell my students the wise thing to do is follow a step-by-step progression, *vinyasa krama*, that lets the body align, stretch, and strengthen safely and in its own time. The students' consistent awareness of connecting breath to mind, breath to body, and mind to body throughout their practice eases the passage of change both internally and externally.

Your work may involve quick decisions in a corporate atmosphere with tough deadlines and even tougher competition. Another person's job may be to get the burger on the bun before the customer starts complaining, still another's might be to see that her client gets the proper workout and strength from her personal training. Regardless of your occupation, if you engage your work with mindful awareness, you're using each moment to its fullest, with little or no waste and no time left to make excuses.

Practice

When the stress of meeting deadlines and fulfilling your work responsibilities becomes overwhelming, close the office door, turn off the telephone, and take a moment to sit quietly with your eyes closed. Step back and observe your thoughts shooting the mental rapids. Focus on exhaling, allowing your breath to carry any tension out of the body. Recite the Tension mantra over and over until you feel a sense of calm and relaxation enter the mind/body.

Tension Mantra

Breathing in, I feel calm.

Breathing out, I let go of all tension.

In this space, let the demands of your schedule align themselves and fall into place. Continue to stay relaxed but awake to what is arising. It is here that you will be able to see what needs to be done first, second, and what will have to wait. Don't rush or push the situation unless you know it can all be done properly. Visualize it as a step-by-step progression, *vinyasa krama,* the natural flow of what you have set into motion. Write down what you have seen, and then get back to work.

Working with Mindfulness

"Because of mindfulness, we see our desires and our aggression, our jealousy and our ignorance. We don't act on them; we just see them. Without mindfulness, we don't see them."

—Pema Chodron

Mike is a yoga teacher and building contractor. One Christmas he gave me the gift of fixing my cantankerous propane wall heater. No sooner was he out the door than the flame would extinguish and I would have to schedule another visit. Each time he returned, he did the job as if for the first time. Regardless of the time it took him to find and replace the faulty part, he remained patient. I asked him how he managed to stay so calm when things go wrong, and he told me that his practice has taught him to surrender to the challenge. He's learned to give up fighting not being able to be somewhere else making more money. His meditation supports his state of mind and allows him to separate himself from the emotions connected to fixing the problem. In his work, there's no choice but to fix the problem. It takes lots of patience, focus, and the ability to forget about everything else.

I put the same question to Jan, a yoga student and corporate worker. She shared with me how going into a crisis situation is just like practicing yoga or meditation. You observe those things that arise and let them go. She removes herself from the situation and lets go of the personal stuff so that she has a clear sense of what is really going on. She cautions against letting yourself get sucked into the emotions of a situation; instead, act only on what you can take care of in the moment. This allows you to be more effective in the workplace. She stressed that there are times in the course of a normal workday when you need to just get away from it all, sit somewhere quiet, and breath.

Mindfulness will help you survive the challenges the workplace forces on you.

Meditation in the workplace is an idea whose time has come. You may not have an office where you can close the door for some privacy, but real life isn't always quiet and tranquil. Learning to focus your mind in the most disruptive situations can teach you a strong lesson.

Practice

Make a commitment to yourself to sit for 10 minutes in the morning and 10 minutes at the end of the day in your place of work. This may mean you arrive earlier and stay later, or carry out your practice amid a bustling warehouse or airport. Sit comfortably wherever you are, close your eyes, and draw your attention away from the external sounds to the rise and fall of your breath. Little by little, the surrounding noise will pass into the background and a sense of calm and well-being will feed into your mind and body.

Use the Focus mantra to stay present to your internal self, where you become no one, not male or female, not human or animal, just pure energy radiating light and peace. Without thinking about it or even knowing it, those around you will be touched in a positive way by your presence in meditation.

Focus Mantra

> *Breathing in,* I quiet my mind.
> *Breathing out,* I disappear.

I have meditated in airports, train stations, on planes and trains, in parks, churches, and at peace demonstrations. Allow the challenge of quieting the mind, while in the midst of activity, help to strengthen and hone your concentration and focus.

Moving Meditation: Midday Respite

The workday is only half over and you wish you were home in the hot tub sipping a martini. Well, some of you might feel that way. The rest of you might wish that either Sean Connery or Catherine Zeta Jones was in that hot tub with you. Others will use their computers for a bit of R&R by checking out the porn sites when the boss isn't looking, shopping online, or checking the latest scores. In other words, your logical mind is overloaded and needs to pass the responsibility over to the creative mind, which easily slips into fantasy mode at times like these.

Instead of slipping into a daydream or surfing on the computer, get up and move, doing what is called, "walking meditation." To learn to walk mindfully, you have to find a quiet spot with a fair distance, at least 30 feet, preferably on a straight, clean, and level path, without anyone around to stare at what you are about to do. Failing this, any distance of up to 10 steps will also do. If you cannot get outside, find a hallway or empty office.

First, stand with your feet hip distance apart and feel your body as it is—the tension, firmness, and natural swaying. Make sure you are relaxed, with a straight posture. Hold or fold your hands together, close your eyes for a moment, and calm your mind. With each exhale, let go of everything you've done that morning. Just be with the present moment in total awareness.

Then, after having gathered your composure, open your eyes and slowly start walking. Direct your gaze forward or rest your eyes on the floor ahead of your feet. Walk freely, at a pace you feel most comfortable and relaxed with. Try to walk at a certain rhythm your mind can latch on to. It will tend to flow along with the rhythm. Then maintain that rhythm for the time being. To help keep your focus, recite the Walking mantra.

Walking Mantra

> *Breathing in,* Right foot, calm.
>
> *Breathing out,* Left foot, relax.

And remember, don't think. Just keep your mind in the present moment. Whenever your attention turns to thoughts, recall your awareness, repeat the mantra, and then return to the footsteps.

When you feel really relaxed, keep your mind keenly aware as it flows along with the footsteps. Be mindful of the sensations in your body—the tension, pulling and pushing forces, the lightness or heaviness of weight, and, finally, the contact of your soles with the ground.

Guided Meditation: Surrender

Chances are very likely that you are going to have days of total burnout when all you want to do is sleep for days on end. Ah, yes, but you don't have the time. Instead, plan for a 20-minute pick me up. You will need …

- A chair with no armrests (a dining chair is fine).
- A folded blanket or small pillow.
- An eye-bag or folded scarf.

Sit on the floor facing the side of the chair. Place the blanket or pillow behind you. Lie back and bring your legs up to rest on the chair seat. Position the blanket or pillow under your head, and cover your eyes with the eye-bag or a folded scarf. Make sure the blanket or pillow under your head is only high enough to support the curve of your neck. Your chin should be slightly lower than your forehead.

If your legs do not rest easily on the chair, bring your knees into your chest, roll over to your side, and gently push yourself up. Adjust the height of your body by using one or more folded blankets. Lie down again and place your legs on the chair seat.

Rest with your arms out to the side, away from your body. Close your eyes and bring your attention to your breath. As thoughts arise and take your attention, recite the Surrender mantra, letting go of all the tension in the body. Lie like this for 10 to 20 minutes, and then roll over to your side and curl into a fetal position, bringing your knees up to your chest and rounding your spine. Using the strength of your arms, push yourself up slowly until you're standing.

Surrender Mantra

Breathing in, I surrender.

Breathing out, I am at peace.

Feel as if the floor is one big sponge absorbing all the tension in your back and shoulders. Give it up, let it go, there's nothing worth holding on to. Be present to the moment and enjoy this time of bliss

Chapter 10

Meditating Your Way
to Carefree Finances

"The key, during both life and death, is to recognize
illusions as illusions, projections as projections, and
fantasies as fantasies. In this way we become free."
—Lama Thubten Yeshe

Even though we know that our attachment to material
riches keeps us from attaining true liberation, we continue to
crave what we cannot have. *If I could just afford a new car
my life will be fine. When I'm finally able to buy a house,
everything will be wonderful. If I could only win the lottery,
I would find true happiness.* After that new car or house is
finally ours, however, we want something else, and the cycle
continues in a never-ending spiral of desire, debt, and anxiety.

Through a daily practice of meditation, you begin to see
how you are asleep to the conditioned nature of your motivations and attachments, how you continually repeat patterns
of thought and behavior that bind you to a narrow, repetitive
life, and mask your true potential.

What we love about money is that we can use it to pay for a roof over our head, food for our table, security in old age, clothes on our backs, and a car for travel. We also use our money to help elevate us above our neighbors, separate us from the poor, and boost our ego.

To earn money, you must exchange energy. The paper has no value in itself; instead, it receives its value from what society decides it is worth. The world cannot function without it, nor should it have to, but how we make and spend our energy exchange can make a difference to our well-being and to our connection to the rest of world.

The Religion of Moneytheism

"... money has become modern man's most popular way of accumulating Being, of coping with our gnawing intuition that we don't really exist."

—David Loy

I'll always remember the first time I encountered the slogan *He who dies with the most toys wins.* At the time, I was going out with a man for whom the slogan seemed to be a personal motto. On our first date, he arrived at my doorstep in his Rolls Royce, thinking I would be thrilled. Instead, he was greeted by my horrified expression. I was more interested in who he was as a human being, not how many material possessions he had. The toys turned out to be a big camouflage, a stand-in for integrity and consideration. It wasn't the first time I encountered money speaking for a person. I was young, living in New York City, and had just begun to explore a practice of meditation. Without knowing it at the time, I had already come to an understanding about money that my meditation practice would confirm in years to come.

In American culture, advertising is based on the premise that greed is good. Although greed is contrary to the ethics and values of most religions, it doesn't really seem to matter much. Given the pervasiveness of greed today, the most widely accepted religion today could be called Moneytheism, the religion of greed.

You may have paused for a chuckle at the absurdity of such a thought, but consider that under the rules of this new religion, the marketplace, instead of being a space for the exchange of goods and services, has become the guiding principle for all nations and people. This new religion functions as a total system with its own dogmas, rituals, and liturgies. It even sends out missionaries to the less-industrialized countries to integrate the people fully into the consumer market of spending money. Can't afford it, no problem—can you say "charge it"?

According to Carolyn Wesson, author of *Women Who Shop Too Much*, "59 million persons in the United States are addicted to shopping or to spending." The number of U.S. shopping centers has grown from 2,000 in 1957 to more than 30,000 today, meaning the number of shopping malls has surpassed the number of high schools in this country.

The problem lies in our attachment to the idea that buying things will bring us happiness. If I only had a new SUV, life would be perfect, so you buy a new SUV, but—surprise—life is not perfect. Why? Because you now have to work harder to make enough money to pay for your new vehicle, your family is upset because you work all the time, and to top it all off our country has to go to war to have enough oil to put into that SUV. Well, your not alone, if that gives you any comfort at all.

When you are in a state of concentrated meditation, where there is just you and the breath, you don't need anything else. You don't have to buy any special clothes or shoes—a simple cushion or folded blanket will serve the purpose. While in a meditating state, you are able to watch your greed arise and pass away, because it exists only if you allow it to. You come to see how buying something on impulse is your reaction to a sudden thought that comes up, and you act on it without first thinking about what you are doing.

When you observe your thoughts in meditation you see how one thought feeds into another, pulling you from focus on the breath to the pair of shoes you wanted to buy, how they will look great with certain pants which might attract your spouse to want a romantic evening. This same fluctuation of the mind happens when you have a cart full of clothes that you want to buy even though you have a closet full of fashionable items already. Meditation shows you how you let your mind lead you, and your mind is filled with images from beautiful full-color advertisements you have seen on TV and in magazines. Some serious mindfulness has been employed in putting those ads together so you, the consumer, will want to be or look like the person in the picture.

Stop Shopping 'til You Drop

Next time you're in the mall ready to buy your fifth pair of blue jeans (and you have three pairs at home you haven't worn yet), take a moment, have a seat, close your eyes, and breathe. Ask yourself …

- Do I really need to buy these jeans?
- Will this purchase make me feel better about myself?
- Is there a better way I can use this money?
- Am I just holding at bay the feeling that there's something missing in my life?

You can even ask yourself these questions before you enter the mall. Is there something better you can be doing with your time than spending money you probably don't even have on goods you probably don't need?

Having money, even a great wealth of money, is not considered wrong or a bad thing, even from the Buddhist perspective. The problems arise when we become a slave to that money. It is when our mental state clings to wanting more and we cannot be happy unless there is a constant increase to our income that we lose our freedom and the money owns us.

The Key Is Nonattachment

"The greatest wealth is contentment."

—Dhammapada

To thrive in a capitalist culture, you must be competitive, ambitious, industrious, and greed-driven. But most men and women just want to be happy, enjoy their families and friends, live a comfortable life, have their needs met, and not have to work 24/7 to have it all. Howard C. Cutter in *The Art of Happiness at Work* mentions that in 2002, *The New York Times* reported that in the past 30 years the real income of Americans has risen over 16 percent, whereas the percentage of Americans who describe themselves as "very happy" has dropped from 36 percent to 29 percent in that same period. And it wasn't just poor people who were unhappy—those with the highest incomes reported the most dissatisfaction!

When Shakyamuni Buddha set off to find a way to end all suffering, he left behind all the riches that a man could ever want. Dancing girls entertained him each night, while he and is buddies hung out eating delicious foods and drinking the best from the king's wine cellar. He had a beautiful wife and child, loving parents, and all the money he could ever possibly need. Yet he knew that it wasn't the *way* to find true happiness. In his heart he felt what every human being comes to feel: Something is missing, something is not complete.

According to Buddhist scholar David Loy, when Shakyamuni found the middle way he discovered that it doesn't simply split the difference between sense-enjoyment and sense-denial. It focuses on calming and understanding the mind, for such insight is what can liberate us from our usual preoccupation with trying to become happy by satisfying our cravings. The goal is not to eliminate all desires, but to experience them in a nonattached way so that we are not controlled by them. Nor does it mean that we must leave the world to learn nonattachment. It calls on us to attain a wisdom that recognizes the true nature of this world, including the true nature of oneself.

The key to liberation is not how much money we have, but how we respond to our situation. The wisdom that develops naturally from nonattachment is knowing how to be content with what we have. When we pursue money just for the sake of having money, we set ourselves on an endless cycle of wanting more, always more. Consequently, we are never satisfied with what we have, and our lives revolve around one goal: the attainment of more money.

This grasping for more wealth throws us out into an unknown future, totally disregarding the present except as a place to sleep and change clothes while on the way to "getting there." Some defined and/or vague goal that drives you to one end—the acquisition of money for the sake of feeling complete, secure, happy, defined, and powerful—keeps you locked in the illusion that true happiness is somewhere out there tied up in thousand dollar bills.

Your meditation practice is merely a way to see the absurdity in missing what's going on around you. Rich and powerful men, when asked on their deathbeds, what they would have changed about there lives, do not say that they wish they had stayed longer at the office. They speak of missed opportunities to see their children grow, moments of love they let slip by, friends they failed to connect with. In the end there is no future. Death is a very present-moment experience.

Meditation can empower your relationship to money in the following ways:

- It makes you aware of whether you shop out of necessity or greed.
- It eases the pain of not having the money you crave.
- It helps you to make choices with clarity and awareness.
- It teaches you to enjoy the pleasure of having money without attachment to wanting more.
- It opens you to acceptance and joy for what you have in the moment.
- It shows you how to let go of your greed and to give generously to others.
- It awakens you to know when you have enough.

Practice

Take a moment to sit quietly. Have your meditation journal nearby so that you can write any insights you might have. Then bring your focus to your breath and count backward, slowly, from 10 to 1, letting go of all tension in your shoulders and lower back. Release the tension in your jaw and facial muscles.

Notice the thoughts that arise concerning money, without engaging them or becoming involved with the emotion they elicit. Ask yourself the following questions:

- Do I make enough money to meet my needs? (This means that your bills are paid, you have a place to live, food to eat, and money for entertainment.)
- How much money do I think will make me happy?
- Do I work just to make money?
- What do I spend my money on?
- How much money do I contribute to help others?
- What is my greatest fear concerning money?

- What would I do if I lost every penny I have?
- What would I do if I won a million dollars?

Write your answers in your meditation journal and then come back to sitting in meditation. Step back and observe the thoughts that come up in relation to your answers. Recite the Money mantra to yourself with each inhale and exhale, to help you put your attachments in perspective, calm your mind, and center your awareness.

Money Mantra

> *Breathing in,* Money comes easily to meet my needs.
>
> *Breathing out,* I let go of clinging to my greed.

Winning the lottery has never proven to ease the suffering of the winner. There are many tragic stories about lottery winners and how their millions only made them more miserable in the end, causing the many who did not win to secretly feel better. In the Dhammapada, Buddha taught that "Fine words or fine features cannot make a master out of a jealous and greedy man. Only when envy and selfishness are rooted out of him may he grow in beauty."

All The Money in the World

"All the happiness there is in this world comes from thinking about others, and all the suffering comes from preoccupation with yourself."

—Shantideva

Not long after the man I was dating took me for a spin in his Rolls Royce, I received an invitation from Maria, a very wealthy woman, to accompany her on her travels to a number of estates she owned in different parts of the world. Looking back, it appears the universe had a few lessons on money and wealth in store for me. I must say that I was excited at the prospect of seeing how the "upper half" lives, and to learn more about this woman as a friend. At the time I was young, naive, and broke, whereas she was in her 40s with seemingly bottomless wealth.

The first leg of our journey took us to Spain, to Maria's newly built villa overlooking the sea. Here I found that all that glitters is not gold. The pea under this *nouveau riche* princess' proverbial mattress turned out to be the age-old problem of finding true love. "Can I trust that someone won't just love me for my money?" she wondered. It seemed as if I had fallen into a segment of *Lives of the Rich and Famous*. Maria was still in court over her most recent boyfriend's spending habits, and had recently taken a fancy to a high-level executive who was trying to make a deal with her father. The emotional dance was filled with intrigue and negotiations that boggled the imagination.

All that money and no one you could trust. Here was incredible power, but none that had anything to do with her as a person; instead, it was all about her money. When we walked into a store to shop, which we did often, the shopkeepers nearly prostrated themselves at Maria's feet in an attempt to please her. While she was in the dressing room, however, I could overhear them gossiping about her, vicious in their intent to tear her down. To her face they showed respect for the power her money represented to them, but behind her back they could assuage their jealousy and greed by dissecting her life.

Dinner served by white-gloved servants were formal affairs with polite conversation, whereas I discovered the workers' kitchen filled with laughter and much bonhomie. In the morning, I would meditate and take long walks around the estates. I found that my practice helped to keep my pleasure-pain cycle balanced. The houses were beautiful and richly decorated, the yacht was basically a small cruise liner that spent most of its time looking good in the harbor. My cravings and desires were going back and forth like a Ping-Pong game. One minute I wanted it all, then the next I saw the pain it caused, then back again to, "Well, maybe just some of it all," then back to wanting to get out of there before I went crazy.

Raised to expect anything money could possibly buy, I was saddened to find the outwardly confident and powerful Maria to be a frightened, paranoid woman trapped by her wealth. She had spent her whole life guarding and protecting her status as a modern-day princess, unable to see the good she could do with the bounty granted her in this lifetime. She had been taught not to give to people because they would just want more. So giving was out. Charities were not considered, and tipping workers was just a waste of cash.

My friend Sati who is an experienced meditator and yogi had traveled with Maria also, so I called to ask how she remembered her experience when confronted with this amount of wealth. "I felt so sad for her when we found out that, indeed, her boyfriend had tried to take her for a ride. I think Maria was a dear person full of the same sets of emotions that most people have, but the huge suitcase full of money she was carrying around altered her life and her experiences considerably. I believe it provided much freedom for her but also a kind of prison. When I was in Spain with her, I felt as if I were also in that prison.

Karmically, inherited wealth signifies good deeds were done in past lives and rewarded in this one. Receiving wealth through honest inheritance can be a wonderful gift to an individual, but how a person uses his or her treasure determines the next cycle of karma. In the spiritual world, this is an opportunity for tremendous growth as a compassionate soul or degeneration through self-indulgence. No matter how much money you have, it cannot keep age at bay, nor stave off the inevitability of death. And no one has ever been able to take it with them when they go.

Living a Generous Life

"Attachment is the mind stuck to an object."

—Lama Zopa Rimpoche

If you're wondering if having all the money in the world will make you happy, I would say that it depends on the individual. According to the Dalai Lama, much depends on the mental state of the wealthy person. "One must train the mind so that you will have no sense of possessiveness or miserliness on your part, that you are able to fully transcend any sense of possessiveness." The scriptures are clear that there must be no clinging to the wealth itself. As long as there is no attachment, no clinging, then "even to own great material resources is not incompatible with the ideal."

Traveling with Maria helped me to realize that I didn't need to be wealthy in order to find contentment in my life. However, I don't think I could have stayed so neutral amid so much opulence had I not been meditating and been taught certain values by my mother. Not a particularly extravagant spender, she always made sure her large family's needs were cared for and there was money left over for others.

I remember one day coming back from the grocery store with my mother driving us. We came to a red light, and a young couple with their three small children crossed the street in front of us. It was obvious from their appearance that they were very poor and possibly hungry as well. My mother reached into her purse, pulled out a $100 bill, and stepped out of the car. Moving quickly over to the corner they had just left, she called out to the family as she made as if to pick something up off the road. The young parents turned to see what the commotion was all about.

"Hello, there, just a minute" my mother said, "you've dropped something." And with that, she swept up to the woman and put the money into her hand. "It must have fallen from one of your pockets," she said, "God bless." Before they knew what had happened, Mom was back in the car, the light turned green, and we sped away. I looked back to see the look of disbelief on those two peoples' faces as they saw what was in their hands.

It wasn't her generosity that impressed me as much as her consideration. She didn't want them to be embarrassed by being offered charity from a stranger. To her the hundred dollars was coming from God, who in His generosity had given it to my mother to share with others.

Practice

There is a practice that says, if you want to attract something to your life, you must first give it away. For example, if you need more time, donate your time to help someone out. If you need more money, give your money to someone who needs it.

Take some time to list in your meditation journal the money you need to attract into your life and exactly how it would be spent. Then check your budget and see how much money you have to give away to a charity, family, or individual who could really use some help financially. Make the donation anonymously. As you sit in meditation, notice what thoughts and emotions arise from taking this action, both before and after you do so. Let all judgments and criticisms pass by without clouding your awareness. Use the Giving mantra to keep you focused on your intention.

Giving Mantra

Breathing in, I give freely.

Breathing out, I open my heart.

Many people make a point of donating 10 percent of their income to charitable causes they believe in, ones they support to make the world a more peaceful place, a world where all children are loved and whose needs are met. It isn't always easy to tithe that money when there are so many luxuries you could buy for yourself and so many bills to pay—especially if you don't have a large income. But what you give comes back to you in ways that only makes your life richer and more positive. It may not always be in the form of paper money, but it will be an exchange of God's deep love for your generosity.

Your Money or Your Life

"Money is something we choose to trade our life energy for."

—Joe Dominguez and Vicki Robin

At age 10, Sally started earning her own money and was thrilled to have the independence to do things that she would normally have to ask her mother to pay for: go to the movies, buy candy and soda pop. Right out of college she got a job teaching special education, even though she really wanted to be working in the theater and studying dance. One evening, as she was stuck in rush-hour traffic going nowhere fast, Sally realized that although she was making a good living and doing honorable work, she was not being true to herself. What she needed to do would bring her very little money, but she would be much happier with her life. So she reduced everything down to the bare necessities, left her job, and opened a children's theater and acting school.

Sally told me that she never wanted her life to be about money, because she felt restricted by the limitations "living just to make money" imposed on her. She credits her meditation practice with giving her the clarity to focus on doing work she loves, work she considers right livelihood, and in return all her financial needs have always been met. I told her that sounded pretty amazing and that most people might find that almost impossible. It requires a great deal of faith and trust in something greater than yourself.

"Not really," she said, "I think of myself as a conduit for God to manifest in the world, then by living my life in service to the others I will get back just what I give." Remember, the law of cause and effect: karma. The important thing is to keep life's possessions to just what is needed, following the middle way. If everybody in this country did that, we could reduce our overspending and overconsumption by more than half.

"Not that I'm so perfect and always succeed," she told me, "but more and more I am able to let go and not give in to spending my money on something I don't really need, something that is only meant to fill the emptiness for a little while. I keep coming back to meditation and to sitting quietly, and bringing calm to my crazy ego/self. Then I can bring my attention back to the present."

Is There More to You Than Your Job Title?

People are so identified with their job title that we judge each other by what we do for a living. Consider how you react when meeting a librarian, a lawyer, or a video-store clerk. Ask yourself the following questions:

- What is your impression of each of these professions?
- Do they tell you anything about the individual person other than the level of his or her pay scale?
- Do you judge the person just by what he or she does for a living?

How Do You Do?

"What do you do for a living?" is usually one of the first things we ask people when we meet them for the first time. Too often, we let people's job title define who they are. The next time you're at a social gathering where you have an opportunity to meet new people, instead of asking them what they do for a living, ask them about their interests, what movies they've seen recently, or whether they have a family. Don't let a person's professional label be the sum total of who he or she is.

My friend Kerry is a very talented and creative artist. He loves to make art, but he also loves watching foreign films. He began helping out at the only video store in town that rented the hard-to-find, director-cut, foreign, and independent films. Kerry soon earned a following with video-store customers, who would rely on his knowledge and judgment when making their rental choices. As if overnight, he became known as a film expert and he came to believe it so strongly that he stopped creating art.

I had been puzzled by his turn around until one morning sitting in meditation I understood what had happened. In listening to what everyone said, Kerry took on the professional label he was given rather than choosing to follow his own path.

As humans we tend to put people, even ourselves, into a mental slot with a title so that, at a glance, we can know how to feel and how to think about a person. As a culture, we are so enamored of labels that we wear them outside our clothes to make a statement about who we are. Designer labels let people in on your financial status, your taste, your hipness, but most of all your willingness to follow the crowd.

Next time you label someone, consider that ...

- Labels are just words we give power to define who we are.
- Labels have nothing at all to do with the true Self.
- Labels help us fit the player to his or her part in our fantasy.
- Labels help us keep our stories of the world in order.
- Labels prevent us from experiencing our true connection to all there is.

Spending for the Right Reasons

"After a day like that, I bought myself a hundred-dollar pair of pink boots to make me feel better."

—Rae Dawn

My friend Dawn loves to celebrate her daughters' birthdays each year with something unique, but in a big way. Yesterday she phoned me, and I could tell from her voice that she was agitated and ready to panic.

When I asked where she was calling from, she said that she was sitting in the back of a long, white, stretch limo, stuck in bumper-to-bumper traffic on a major highway in a snowstorm. With her were five 15-year-old girls.

"There were supposed to be eight girls altogether," she yelled over the background noise of their laughter, "but they couldn't all make it at the last minute. So now I have this huge car, a driver who doesn't speak English, who's gotten lost three times, got stuck in a ditch, hit a Christmas tree, and ran over a pole. But the worst part is that the girls are just ignoring me."

She called me the next day asking for the name of a massage therapist who could fit her in on short notice. Engrossed in writing this chapter on finances, I asked her how much money it cost her for all this agitation. "Well, the limo was $560, the tip another $112, dinner was $120 for all of us. After a day like that, I bought myself a pair of hundred-dollar pink boots to make me feel better. And now I'm going to spend $65 on a massage to help me recover. Financially, I really had to bite the bullet on this one."

For almost a thousand dollars, Dawn was able to secure a good time for her daughter and her friends at the mall, have dinner, and return home stressed, agitated, and angry at everyone and almost everything that happened. She had a picture of how it all would turn out, that somehow the great joy she brought her daughter would be worth the financial price. Dawn and her husband are good people who work hard and are grateful for all they have. Can you recognize yourself in Dawn's story?

Our society is designed in such a way that our spending drives the machine. Our money keeps people in jobs, keeps corporations running the world, and the free market open and flowing. Credit fosters debt that many people cannot pay their way out from under. Families such as Dawn's are fortunate to have the money to spend on a day out at the shopping mall. But what if you're poor and can barely make ends meet? If you are strapped for cash, hearing Dawn's story might make you feel angry or jealous for what she did. It may be that you and your spouse fight over how to spend every penny, while your children go to bed hungry at night. You don't care if money is good or bad, you just want some.

Your meditation practice can help to bring you some insight into how much your life is run by having enough money. Consider some of the ways you think about money and how meditation can help shift your perspective:

- When your whole life is about not having money, the world around you forces you to think about it all the time.

  In meditation, you find a rest from the constant onslaught of thoughts about needing money.

- When you have more than enough money and you still want more, you're being greedy.

  In meditation you see your greed for what it is, bringing balance to your craving.

- When you have very little money and you want enough to meet your needs, you're looking out for yourself.

  In meditation you come to know what brings you joy and contentment.

For those of you who have money but remember a time when you had none, what owned you then? Every penny was precious, every dollar thought out before buying something. Money constituted energy, it was precious and relevant to your life. Without mindful awareness, we become spoiled and jaded, spending without conscious thought for where the products come from, how many forests were cut down, how much of our pristine land was ravaged, how many children work long hours to make us happy for just a few minutes of pleasure.

Practice

Sit in meditation, bring your awareness to the breath, and relax the tension in your body and mind. Slowly count to six on the inhale and count to eight on the exhale. Repeat this for six rounds. As thoughts come up, pay them no attention and continue to count your breath.

At the end of the six rounds of breath, relax and breathe normally. Notice any emotions that came up after reading the preceding section.

Ask yourself …

🖋 Do I spend my money without thinking about what I am buying?

🖋 Am I influenced by what is being shown on television?

🖋 Do I wear designer labels so people will think better of me?

🖋 Do I live beyond my means?

🖋 Can I pay off my debts within a short period of time?

🖋 Do I use mindful awareness when spending money?

Life Mantra

Breathing in, Money is energy.

Breathing out, My life is sacred.

In meditation you come to see the sacredness of all life. When we trade our life energy for money, we have the power to do great things for ourselves and for others. Let your practice guide you through your desires and cravings, let it be a calm beacon of light.

You Get What You Give

greedy   1. Desiring more than one needs or deserves. 2. Having too strong a desire for food and drink.

—*Webster's New World Dictionary*

In mindful meditation, you more easily see yourself holding on when you need to open your hand and let go. It takes practice to develop a giving nature, but as you do so it becomes easier to let go of your attachments. After awhile your mind naturally begins to think of others before yourself. When you give to others you generate the cycle of energy that works like a boomerang. What you send out comes back to you, both in thought and action.

Depictions of the Buddhist wheel of life show three animals—a pig, a snake and a rooster—which symbolize the mental afflictions of greed, hatred, and delusion. These three afflictions are said to stem from our fundamental ignorance and are also responsible for the negative acts that we commit as we journey through life. The task is to destroy each of them in our quest for liberation. The practice of meditation, while leading a moral life and following the noble eightfold path, is said to be the means of achieving this goal.

In meditation we can see these afflictions in ourselves, in the whole of society, and even among nations. Because of them, our sense of reality is unstable and unclear. They cause us to judge what we see according to our likes and dislikes, attractions, and aversions. Meditation gives us the space to transcend these emotions and see what is real in the moment. When the Buddha taught that all beings are worthy of respect and love, whether we like them or not, he spoke of these three mental demons, and how we can transform them:

- Greed becomes generosity.
- Hatred becomes loving kindness and compassion.
- Delusion becomes wisdom.

Meditation opens us to respect life, to give as an antidote to greed, to feel compassion and loving kindness in place of hatred. We take noble action when we share what we have with those in need, when we think kindly of those who have hurt us. Such noble action is not always easy— greed and hatred are deeply rooted in most of us and it takes constant vigilance to note how they can arise in one's daily life unbidden and to deal with such impulses before they can take effect.

Generosity and giving helps to break the cycle of attachment to that which you cannot release, to that which will not release you. When it is so hard to let go, ask yourself what is the worst thing that could happen if you surrender your attachment to money and share what you have with others. Go through all the arguments, write them down in your meditation journal, and look at them in the honest light of your present reality. You will see that there is always money to be made and it will come and go like the tides of the sea, like the thoughts in your mind, just like your cravings and desires. Let them all go by, keeping your hands open to receive, rather than your fists closed in struggle.

Moving Meditation: Conscious Investing

If you invest your money in the stock market, take some time to look over your portfolio and learn more about the companies your money goes to support.

As in all other aspects of your life, you should follow the precepts of nonharming, nonstealing, and right conduct when you invest your money. Know whether you hold shares in chemical companies that poison the environment, biotech companies that alter the gene strains of our food, or manufacturers who make weapons for war. There are a number of reputable investment companies willing to help you make socially responsible investments.

Socially responsible investing (SRI) integrates personal and social values with investment decisions and recognizes the fact that providing capital to companies in effect endorses their activities. Social investors realize that although they may have limited control over the use of their tax dollars, they have much greater control over their investment dollars and what they want to support with them.

When you sit in meditation, let your mind calm. Let your fears and questions arise and pass away. As you learn to live in the moment, know that it is okay to plan for your future needs by investing your money in companies that will ensure the health and well-being of the planet. Remember that it's the quality of our actions when spending money that determines its positive or negative effects on all beings.

Conscious Mantra

> *Breathing in,* The money I invest
> *Breathing out,* Helps to shape the world.

Recite this mantra to help strengthen your resolve when investing money or looking to change your stocks from one company to another. How we care for the world determines the health and welfare of all beings, including yourself.

Guided Meditation: Your Most Valuable Possession

Take a moment to walk through your house or apartment, staying fully present to what you see around you. Notice what you have in each room and, without judgment or criticism, mentally note what is necessary to have for your life to function properly and what is unnecessary clutter.

You might decide that you cannot live without any of your posses-sions, or you might see an accumulation of objects that you don't need.

Now sit on a chair or meditation cushion and bring your attention to your breath. Allow your mind to calm and relax slowly. Allow yourself to come into the present moment aware that without your breath there is no life to be had, no possessions to own, no money to be made.

The most simple activity, we perform every second of every day is the most important thing that we have. You could lose everything else and it would not matter, as long as you have *prana*—your breath and your life.

Value Mantra

Breathing in, There is life.

Breathing out, I am content.

Recite the Value mantra and let your breath arise without any help from you, just observe the wondrous way in which your mind and body are fueled by a simple inhale and exhale.

Chapter 11

Abundance and Prosperity

"You are prosperous to the degree that you are experiencing peace, health, and plenty in your world."
—Catherine Ponder

Walk into a bookstore and you'll find any number of books extolling the possibility of attaining abundance and prosperity. Mostly, they deal with attracting more money or more material possessions, as if having this kind of abundance means that you have achieved a higher level of prosperity. The true meaning of *abundance* and *prosperity* is lost to those who perceive money and possessions as of utmost importance, however. Meditation points us within, to find genuine abundance and prosperity, and the treasures we find within are determined by the quality of our thoughts.

One thing that these books have in common with your meditation practice is training the mind to think clearly, to stay focused and maintain a positive outlook in life. They extol the concept that living in the present creates the future, and that you manifest results in your life from the quality of your thoughts.

This explains why some people have so much more than others. It seems unfair that there are people who get everything they want while others, with the same talents and intelligence, can never seem to get ahead. There is enough for everyone to live a prosperous, healthy life—plenty of food to feed the hungry, medicine to heal the sick, resources to house the homeless, and experience to know that war only breeds more war.

As the spiritual philosopher Anon tell us, "All the power and energy of the whole universe resides within you. All of the Infinite Intelligence is present at any point in the universe. It makes no difference how many individuals the energy is flowing through; there is always an inexhaustible supply. You are the heir to all the energy there is, for there are no divisions in Infinity. You are the recipient of all the riches, power, and wisdom of the Infinite."

Anon isn't just talking about making a few more dollars to cover the rent. What he is saying is that there is plenty for everyone, that there is enough abundance, when we know how to tap into what is available to us. Your meditation practice is particularly important in recognizing this abundance because it trains your mind to control your thoughts, which direct the actions you will take. When you can find peace and acceptance within yourself, you can better monitor your destructive emotions and stay mindful that you are a spiritual being on an evolutionary path.

Success in all other aspects in your life depends on your ability to live an abundant and prosperous life. Why? Because prosperity is all about what you think, the quality of your thoughts, and how they are made manifest in the world. This relates to all areas of your life:

- More abundant love in your relationships
- A natural progression to financial prosperity
- A letting go of fear to allow for abundance
- An abundance of patience and tolerance
- Greater health and well-being
- Abundant creativity
- Prosperity in your work life

The Reality of Abundance and Prosperity

"As a man thinketh within himself, so is he."

—Proverbs 23:7

Everyone knows someone who is a chronic complainer. Nothing is ever right, they are never happy no matter what they do or what is done for them. They live in a world of negativity and no possibility. When you ask whether he or she would like to do something that you consider fun, the first word out of his or her mouths is "no."

"Hey, honey, why don't we take a walk in the park today. The sun is out, the flowers are starting to bloom, and it would be nice to get out for some fresh air."

"No, it's too cold, and anyway, my back's been giving me some problems. I've gotta take care of the bills that I slave each week to pay off, so you go ahead, I'll just stay here and get some work done."

Do I exaggerate? Maybe for some, but not for all of you. The "No Person," I call them. Without even considering the positive side of a situation, they jump head first into what is wrong and lacking.

Overflowing with Good Fortune

The word "abundance" comes from *abunda-re*, Latin for "to overflow." "Prosperity" comes from the Latin *prospera-re*, meaning "to render fortunate."

The mind is like a river that can flow in any direction. Using meditation, you can train the mind to flow smoothly in a certain direction— of your choice. You can choose to have an abundance of "no" mind or prosper with a mind that you guide to live fully in the moment, free of any lack or desperation.

Abundance is a state of mind, and prosperity is the result of how your mind functions. You don't have to spend your days saying one money affirmation after another to attract it into your life. In the *Tao of Abundance*, Laurence G. Boldt instructs us that "material abundance will come not from struggling to attain it as a goal in itself, but rather as a natural by-product of experiencing a deeper state of psychological abundance."

Your meditation practice will reveal to you ...

- That there is nothing you have to do.
- That your thoughts create your reality.
- That you resist the flow of abundance in your life.
- That abundance and prosperity are already there for you to have.

The Unconscious Mind

Right now you're probably sitting there thinking, "If it is all there already and there's nothing for me to do, then why do I feel there's something lacking? Where is all this abundance and prosperity hiding out?" Actually it hasn't been hiding out at all, it's just been waiting for you to wake up to what has been there, within you, all along. Meditation allows you to clear away the veil of ignorance and see how your mind works so you can begin to manifest your tremendous potential for abundance and prosperity.

According to *Time* magazine, Richard Davidson, a researcher at the University of Wisconsin at Madison, has been using brain imaging to show that meditation shifts activity in the prefrontal cortex (the area directly behind our foreheads) from the right hemisphere to the left.

The negative "no" people are right-brain prefrontal oriented, whereas those individuals who are left-brain prefrontal dominant tend to be happier, more enthusiastic, relaxed, and filled with the joy of life. It is in this state of mind that you naturally reside with the flow of universal abundance and prosperity. What this suggests is that a regular practice of meditation can reorient the brain from a stressful fight-or-flight mode to one of acceptance, a significant shift that increases contentment.

As you come to know how your brain works, you begin to see how it all plays out through the functions of your mind. What is visible to you in your initial thinking is just one layer or realm, from which you comprehend what is taking place around you.

Practice

Use your meditation journal to write your answers to the following questions:

- Is your first response to a situation usually negative?
- Do you feel there is never enough in your life?
- Do you feel that everyone else has more opportunities than you do?
- Do you feel that you lack the power to move forward in your life?
- Do you always have an excuse for not having enough 1) Money, 2) Energy, 3) Love, 4) Happiness, 5) Talent, 6) Patience?

After you've answered the questions, sit in meditation and allow your mind to calm. Bring your focus to your breath and let go of any tension in your body. Allow the exhale to "clean house," removing the toxic buildup of stress and negativity in your mind. Mentally step aside so that as the thoughts arise you are simply observing your ego/mind reacting to what is momentarily present. Recite the Abundance mantra to dissolve the negative thoughts and release the internal light of mindful awareness.

Abundance Mantra

Breathing in, Abundance surrounds me.

Breathing out, Abundance is life.

Your mental illusions conspire to have you believe that there is lack and scarcity in your life. To dissolve them, you must first be aware of what you are doing. As author and Yoga teacher Godfrey Devereux says, "We must first recognize our limitations before we can change them."

Following the Path of Abundance

"Train your senses to be obedient. Regulate your activities to lead you to the goal. Hold the reins of your mind as you hold the reins of wild horses."

—Svetasvaara Upanishad 11.9

What more could you want than what you already have? What more is there to have than what is contained in this very moment: you, with this book in your hands, reading about how to have more if only you could find the time to meditate. The trouble is that when you do finally sit for a few minutes your mind is so jumpy you think that you might as well be getting something else done. Putting yourself into the natural ebb and flow of the stream of prosperity can be difficult work.

Years ago I recited affirmations, one after the other, in hopes of changing the perpetual tape loop of how I saw myself. Many self-help books use them to direct the mind in a positive direction, but as I went through the exercises I noticed that there was something deeper missing. I was only exchanging one way of thinking for another. My mind was still running at a hundred miles an hour, without any real focus. Instead, when a negative thought popped into my head, I quickly recited an opposite affirmation.

To the degree that I was able to recognize my negative thinking, this form of work was beneficial. Affirmations have helped many people to change their lives for the better. But the truth behind the mental afflictions—the attachment to pleasure and pain, the endless cycle of mental acrobatics—was not addressed until I began to sit in meditation and, with mindful awareness, bring the whole shebang into focus.

The discipline of meditation is learned throughout one's lifetime, not just a two-week seminar that will liberate your monkey mind.

In the beginning of your meditation practice you learn to focus the mind, but over time you begin to internalize this focus. This involves the senses, taste, touch, sight, and sound detaching from their objects and losing their power over the mind. As you would take the reins of the wild horse and bring it under control, this form of focus tames your undisciplined senses. You come to know your senses in the true meaning of abundance and prosperity—mindfully aware of the plenty you have been given while acknowledging with gratitude how truly fortunate you are to be alive. In meditation, this deep focus prevents your distraction from the external stimuli of your senses. You'll begin to ...

- Taste your food with awareness, finding the abundance of subtle layers and dimensions in each bite you take.
- Feel another person's touch on your skin, the rub of fabric against the flesh, a chill wind against your face.
- Appreciate the smell of roses in bloom, a newborn baby, the sea at sunrise, the city in a traffic jam.

- Notice the beauty of what your eyes see every day—a passing smile, the majesty of a tree, the formation of icicles on a rain pipe, the shadow of a hawk flying overhead.

- Hear the ever-present sounds of the world going by—leaf blowers on a fall afternoon, a woman laughing, a child crying, coyotes howling at the moon, your heart beating in anticipation.

In your daily life of staying present, you can be awake to what is happening around you; in the moment of meditation, however, you withdraw the senses through the mindful internalization of your breath. You must first acknowledge your senses before you can begin to bring them under control.

The Bhagavad Gita tells us ...

"The world of the senses gives rise to heat and cold, pleasure and pain.

"They come and they go and do not last. Bear them patiently.

For a person unmoved by these changes, for whom sorrow and happiness are the same is truly wise, and fit for immortality."

The Life Stream

"Concentration is to bind consciousness to a single spot."

—Patanjali

With the withdrawal of your senses, you can then begin to fully concentrate. The sage Patanjali, who wrote the Yoga Sutras, says that concentration is the beginning of meditation, whereas meditation is the culmination of concentration. Concentration is the binding of the mind to one place, object, or idea. Mentally you are totally absorbed in the object of your attention. You are further training the monkey mind to stay still, to be fixed on one point.

Your concentration can come to rest on the idea of awakening you to God's great abundance and prosperity in your life. It is already there, but your concentration brings it to life so that it may manifest fully. You have but to see it in your mind's eye and, like with a caged bird, open the door and let it fly.

Mary prays for her family every day. At 83 years old, she practices meditation in her prayer life, bringing her concentration to the object, asking for a resolution, and trusting God to take care of it. Sometime ago it came into her mind to pray for communication and affection between her son, Ian, and daughter, Peggy. Ian spent every Sunday at Peggy's house, watching football and eating Peggy's food. He came over empty-handed and never offered to reciprocate for her hospitality.

Mary sat in meditation and, using the concentration of her mind, asked for his heart to be opened with abundant love and then handed it over to God. A few days later, Peggy's car broke down and no shop could fix it. Each morning Ian picked Peggy up and took her to work, then again in the evening brought her home. He went out and bought the parts for the car, hired a mechanic, and paid to have it repaired. The abundance of love that rested just below the surface was drawn forth by Ian's actions.

Mary told me that you must trust that what you pray for will manifest. Many people have no faith in themselves, they are afraid that their intention will not be taken seriously. "I simply give it to the Lord and ask Him to take care of it. The key is really to trust. God has said, I am within you. Carry me and give me to others. All the good that exists is our Divine right. All you have to do is ask."

Concentration can direct your thought energy out into the world to manifest an intention, as in the case of Mary, or it can be brought to the one pointed beam of light directed deeper into the still point of meditation.

Practice

To begin a practice of concentration, it would be helpful to have an object, such as a candle flame, a flower, or something that represents the idea you wish to have manifest.

Sit in a meditative posture and bring your focus to the object in front of you. To keep your concentration, focus on the brightness of the flame, and then shift your concentration to any positive feelings surrounding what you are asking for.

After awhile, close your eyes and bring the image into your mind. Try to hold it there. When you lose it, open your eyes and see the object again. The point of this practice, called *tradak*, is to grasp the object in your mind and not let it go.

Stay with it. When you become frustrated and want to quit, recite the Perseverance mantra with each breath until you are calm again. Then bring your concentration back to the object.

Perseverance Mantra

Breathing in, My mind is running.

Breathing out, I bring it back.

It is very difficult for the mind to maintain a focus on something abstract or to visualize a situation, because the mind tends to be so easily distracted and wander off to some other train of thought. For instance, as you gaze at the flame, maybe it reminds you of a candle-light dinner you shared with an old lover. Before you know it, you are remembering the romantic evening instead of holding the image of the candle flame in your mind. This is how the unfocused mind works; you must train it with patience and understanding.

Divine Manifestation

"At the still point of the turning world ... at the still point there the dance is."

—T. S. Eliot

Now you are at the heart of the practice, meditation, where the mind is fixed and communication between the meditator and object of meditation is steady. Swami Satchidananda describes it as one continuous stream of oil poured from one pot to another. There is no break in the flow. Time has no meaning in meditation, and all sense of space is lost. You may sit down to meditate at 8 A.M. and, an hour later, open your eyes, feeling as if only a few minutes have passed. On the other hand, you may sit for 10 minutes and it feels like an hour of struggle. The first example describes how time disappears when you are in deep meditation, while the second exemplifies the mind's struggle to focus and concentrate on the continuous passing of time.

This deep interpenetration brings you closer to what the yogi's call the final limb on the yogic path, *samadhi*. Here it becomes difficult to describe in words because nobody can consciously practice samadhi. Up to this point all your efforts have gone into practicing how to concentrate. In meditation you have the meditator, the meditation, and the object meditated upon and at this point it becomes effortless, you are just there, although you know you are in meditation. Now here is where it gets difficult to grasp. In samadhi there is neither the object nor the meditator. The one pointed focus of concentration, knowing you are in meditation, shifts into you not being there to know it because you and God are one. This is liberation. This is enlightenment. In samadhi there is no me, mine, or I. There just is.

Your Life Values

"If we do not accept the idea that we 'deserve' to prosper, then even when abundance falls in our laps, we will refuse it somehow".

—Louise L. Hay

When Donna, a very attractive brunette with big dark eyes, came to a yoga class she had a tension in her body like a tightly wound spring. She carried a great deal of anger, was alienated from her family, and had been fired from one job after another. Her practice became her lifeline. On the yoga mat she was fully present and enjoyed the process. Over the years, I watched her conquer one fear after another until, finally, she confronted her mental afflictions.

Her conversation about herself had always been "why me?" She attracted negative people and situations and mentally blocked the flow of any abundance and prosperity. She persevered in her practice, training her mind to focus, to concentrate, to see that the "why me?" was because of "me." She was her own worst enemy, her fears kept her from moving forward, her anger put a wall around her, and her illusions kept her from seeing what was really happening.

Then one day she had a breakthrough. I've seen this happen before in both yoga and sitting meditation, where something will shift. For years some will resist doing a headstand out of fear, and then it happens, with ease. They were ready for it. They do what they could never do before, they allow themselves to receive the natural flow of abundance that is their due.

If it happens while sitting in meditation, it can be an instant of total clarity, where the mind, the body, the world falls away and all that resides is pure energy, alive and free of all shackles. What a moment! You have had a glimpse past the veil, and in that instant you have inhaled the breath of God. There is no going back from there. There is only standing in the stream of love in full awareness that all the abundance of the universe is there to be shared.

In a single moment, after years of practice, Donna understood. She saw her anger, her fear, and gave up the struggle. She just let it go. Since then, much has changed in her life. She told me how close she has gotten to her family for the first time in her life. She decided to start her own business and is making more than she ever made working for someone else. She is joyful and content to be herself, and she credits her practice with her mental transformation.

It is our ways of thinking that block the flow of prosperity. When you recognize this, you will be able to see the path that will help dissolve your mental barriers. In this world of abundance, the emptiness you feel—the emptiness you fill with thoughts about more money, clothes, jewelry, love, more about the "I," the "me"—is your longing for connection to the Divine. Stop using God as a reason for your failures. With God within, your Divine right is to be prosperous, to be supported by abundance, so that you can walk the spiritual path without the mental distractions of constantly clinging to wanting more.

In the words of philosopher James Allen, "Through his thoughts, man holds the key to every situation and contains within himself that transforming and regenerative agency by which he may make himself what he wills."

Practice

Where does one begin to transform lack into abundance? You really don't have to wait years for the stream to move your way. You are already standing waist deep. Now leave the shore and take a swim. You can begin with your meditation practice and follow these 10 steps for opening your heart and mind to receiving more abundance and prosperity into your life.

1. Sit in meditation and quiet your mind. Bring your concentration to what you seek, such as abundant health, financial prosperity, or more love in your family.

2. Ask whether there is any reason why you should not receive what is rightfully yours to have. Clear away any doubts from your mind. Allow yourself to open to possibility rather than holding to a negative attitude.

3. After you have decided to accept the prosperity, and it feels right for you to have, make a mental picture of the highest degree of it that you wish to experience. For instance, if it is financial well-being that you seek, mentally imagine the amount of income you wish to have and build a picture of your financial wealth working in your life—the home you will have, the good you will do with it, the experiences you will have.

4. Make sure you're mental picture is what you really want and not what someone else thinks you should have. This is your life, and the gift of abundance should support your path. If you are not sure what constitutes enough, adhere to the middle way, that all your immediate needs will be met: bills paid, food to eat, house for you and your family.

5. Do not dissipate your vision for your life by telling others. Keep it to yourself. Speaking your intention before it manifests can weaken it by what other people have to say about it, or their doubts and jealousies can influence your positive mindset.

6. Begin to take the first steps toward your intention. Set a time limit and plan to achieve certain things within six months, others within a year, and others within two years. Keep notes in your meditation journal, writing down what you would like to achieve, when, and how.

7. Each day use a part of your meditation to concentrate on your intention. If things do not happen as quickly as you would like, stay calm and allow the power of Divine energy to work in its own time. Try not to force or rush what must be revealed step-by-step.

8. Realize that your dreams have already come true on the mental plane and are moving out into the world and coming back to you. What you think is what you attract, so accept that this is the best thing for you.

9. When you question or doubt that anything will happen for you, look around and see that others have attained great things in their lives from thinking, visualizing, and taking action to make their dreams come true. Observe someone who has done or is doing what you want to do, find out how that person accomplished his or her goals, and model your actions on his or hers. Why reinvent the wheel?

10. Continuously reaffirm that everything already exists in the world of substance. With the power of your mind, you can bring forth your heart's intentions. Meditate each day to renew your focus, clarify your intentions, and see yourself in the light of God's love.

Seeding Mantra

Breathing in, I grow my life from the seeds that I plant.

Breathing out, I plant love, generosity, compassion, and kindness.

Take care that what you seek is compassionate with all other beings in the world.

The Joy of Prosperity

"The greatest revolution of my life is the discovery that individuals can change the outer aspects of their lives by changing the inner attitudes of their minds."

—William James

Abundance is God's love, and within that resides everything. As you come to understand your connection to what Patanjali calls "the infinite beyond duality," you glimpse that you are already enlightened, it is not something that can be manufactured, it is already there. It is exactly because of our separateness, our denial of oneness with all other elements in the universe, that we delude ourselves with the concept of lack. Amazing as it may seem, it is as if you were surrounded with anything and everything you could possibly need—shelter, food, money, love, material goods, compassion, kindness, protection—and you won't see it, won't accept that it is simply there for you to have.

The power of your meditation practice resides in revealing that there is nothing to fear. All the fears that you have are groundless in the light of God's love within you. J. Krishnamurti says that when you are inspired by your meditation practice, your thoughts break free, your mind transcends its limitations, your consciousness expands in every direction, and you find yourself in a new, great, and wonderful world: the world of abundance and possibility. Forces, faculties, and talents that once lay fallow spring to life, and you discover yourself to be a greater person by far than you ever dreamed yourself to be.

When coming to these realizations, the greatest support we can have is mindfulness, which means being totally present in each moment. When your mind remains centered, there are no stories to make up, no mental agitations to distract you, there is just the moment, and in that space there is room for nothing else. In that emptiness there is everything. We don't have to think, imagine, or wonder about it; we sit in nonjudgment absorbed in knowing.

Debra's Practice

I asked my friend Debra how her meditation practice has influenced her beliefs about abundance and prosperity. She wrote back to say that "if we accept the fact that the conscious mind takes its cues from what is lingering in our deep belief systems, then I would say that my lifestyle reflects my feelings pretty accurately."

Debra continued:

> I have never been very materialistic or paid too much attention to money. At the same time, I have been able to do many things that usually require a lot of money. I have traveled and lived in other places, I feel comfortable and safe in my living space and find an aesthetic appreciation of it. It is simple but lovely.

I feel all my basic needs are more than taken care of. I have never felt comfortable with extreme wealth. I look at it and it sickens me to a certain degree. I'm talking, I guess, about what the media shows us, people who spend such huge quantities of money on clothes, housing, and gobbling up all the land around them. I, personally, wouldn't have taken this on ... therefore, I did not attract it into my life.

I do ask for abundance in my prayer meditation, but I also believe that it can take many forms, so I don't want to be too specific with the universe. As I grow older, I must admit, I tend to think of money as some kind of security but against what, I'm not sure. This is part of my current examination—do I want more money in the upcoming years?

I have found that the things I really needed have come to me without too much aggravation on my part. I remember in my late 30s when I realized very clearly that I needed a job—I sent that message to my subconscious very strongly and a few months later I had the teaching position I still hold after 20 years. I haven't tried this frivolously and perhaps because I have never asked for anything over the top, I have always gotten what I needed.

Debra's practice showed her the middle way was how she felt most comfortable in living her life. The Buddha taught that it is up to you to find your way, that the books and great teachers only point you in the right direction. Meditate on his words from the Dhammapada:

But if you meditate
And follow the law
You will free yourself from desire.
Everything arises and passes away.
When you see this, you are above sorrow.
This is the shining way.
Existence is sorrow.
Understand, and go beyond sorrow.
This is the way of brightness.
Existence is illusion.
Understand, go beyond.

This is the way of clarity.
Master your words.
Master your thoughts.
Never allow your body to do harm.
Follow these three roads with purity
And you will find yourself upon the one way,
The way of wisdom.

Moving Meditation: The Prosperity Dance

Create a space in your room in which you can move with freedom. Push the furniture against the walls and pick up anything on the floor that might get in your way.

Choose some music that speaks to your sense of rhythm and put it on to play. Now stand in the center of your space and listen to the sounds of the instruments as they unfold the notes of music. Allow your body to pick up the rhythm and begin to move your body in any way that feels the best.

It doesn't matter if you've never danced before—surrender to the moment and let go of all your restrictions, all your reasons for why you cannot dance, and let the music carry you around your space as if you were as light as a feather.

Bring your attention to the strength of your legs, those same legs that carry you through each day obedient to your every whim. Notice how your arms extend as you lift them into the air, feel the gyration of your hips as they respond to the beat of the drums, your spine following every twist and turn.

This is abundance; and you carry it with you from the moment you are born. With this body comes a mind that hears the music through ears poised to receive sound, a voice that communicates the depths of your thoughts. With this instrument, human beings have been able to create their own world, their fortunes, their destiny.

The body that moves you in this dance and the mind that focuses on your movements are offered the same opportunities as everyone else. Take advantage of them.

Prosperity Mantra

Breathing in, I accept the best that life has to offer.

Breathing out, I manifest the best in the here and now.

Guided Meditation: The Abundance of Life

Sit on a cushion with your legs crossed in front of you or on a straight-backed chair and bring your awareness to your breath.

Allow your thoughts to arise and pass as you focus on the flow of inhale and exhale. Silently give thanks for what you have been given in your life, including all the good and painful lessons that have made you the person you are today.

Acknowledge with gratitude all the opportunities that have been presented to you in the past, accepting that there are always more still to come.

Surrender to the stillness of the moment, knowing that the most precious gift you have is your life, and each passing second a treasure to be discovered.

Thankful Mantra

Breathing in, I am grateful for life's abundance.

Breathing out, May all beings be prosperous.

Remember that it is not always possessions that bring us the greatest happiness. The most free and powerful individuals are those who could be happy with the fewest things.

Chapter 12

The Meaning of Life:
A Sense of Purpose

"When we practice looking deeply, we have the insight into what to do and what not to do for the situation to change. Everything depends on our way of looking."
—Thich Nhat Hanh

Wake up! There's more to your life than what you see on the surface. It may be subtle, outrageous, dangerous, or extremely difficult, but the thread that binds you to each lifetime is made up of specific lessons for you to learn—not just lessons to learn, but actions to be carried out, deeds to be accomplished, illusions to be dissolved in the light of understanding. And not every life is the same as another. We all have our parts to play on this ever-rotating Earth stage, one feeding into another into another.

Looking inward with mindfulness brings you to an understanding of your purpose on this planet. The true gaze of modern civilization is blind; its faculties of judgment are impaired and blocked by fantasy and illusion. What George Ohsawa has to say about philosophy applies equally to meditation: "Without a practical technique, philosophy becomes useless, while at the same time a technique without a guiding principle is absurd and often dangerous." It is the practical technique that supports the traditional meditation teachings brought to us from the East; and when used as merely an escape from the world, it can prove to be dangerous. Generally, if you make good use of your mind, skill, and talent in your lifetime, you will feel like you've found and fulfilled your purpose. If you make good use of your time, this, too, will give you a feeling of accomplishment for your life's work. Consider that one in a thousand individuals ever puts his or her time to anywhere near its potential good use—not time spent thinking about the past or the future, but time spent living full on in the moment. Living fully in the present is being "true to yourself" by taking control of your mind and accepting responsibility for your actions.

In *The Mind and the Way*, Ajahn Sumedho writes, "Everything is as it is. It has no name other than the name we give it. It is we who call it something; we give it a value. We say this thing is good or it's bad, but in itself, the thing is only as it is. It's not absolute; it's just as it is. People are just as they are."

It may be that on closer examination, despite your dull job, difficulty in maintaining a relationship, or lack of financial support, you are carrying out your life's purpose by just *being* right where you are. The quality of your existence depends on whether you express compassion, generosity, and loving kindness in your actions with those around you. As Ram Dass says, "Be here now" and find the way to live your passion exactly where you are in this moment.

The Stages of Life

"All the world's a stage, and all the men and women merely players. They have their exits and their entrances, and one man in his time plays many parts, his acts being seven ages."

—William Shakespeare, *As You Like It*

"At first the infant mewling and puking in his nurses arms ..." Thus begins the soliloquy in which Shakespeare tells the story of the cycles of a man's life. He calls them seven stages, each one different from the other, a progression through time toward inevitable death. No matter how you arrange them, they all head in the same direction. At each juncture of your life, there will be a shift and, if you are awake enough, it will call for a reexamination of where you have come from and where you go next. Meditation gives you the clarity to see the truth of your actions, to deal with them with *satya* (honesty) and *ahimsa* (without harm).

Let's examine the different stages of life when combined with a daily practice of meditation.

Childhood

The ability to sit quietly, reflect, and concentrate is the cornerstone for developing a meditation practice; this is hard enough for adults to accomplish, much less the active mind of a child.

In *Teaching Meditation to Children,* David Fontana and Ingrid Slack write that, due to the speed in which our society is constantly changing, the nature of right and wrong becomes blurred, leaving children with insufficient guidance as to how they should live their lives and think about their own being. The fact that we live in a world of extreme materialism promotes the afflictions of greed and attachment, already inherent in our natures, but overemphasized when combined with massive marketing campaigns. Meditation gives children the chance to step away from the constant onslaught of messages and images and to sit quietly. In meditation children discover more positive feelings about themselves and the nature of their actions. It teaches them early that material possessions provide only transient, temporary pleasures and that love and kindness can bring lasting pleasures.

Teen Years

Today's teenagers have been exposed to more information, deaths, violence, and sexual experiences than any previous generation. Their young minds have been pushed fast and aggressively toward the grown-up world, without giving them enough time to make the transition step by step. They are on the fast track—too fast—with no limits set to contain the momentum of their speeding thoughts.

When these speeding thoughts come up against the practice of still-ness, teens often recognize in the stillness their need for balance and calm. When teaching meditation to teenagers, I have always found them to respond with gratitude. Here, at last, is a place to rest and find some peace. Meditation gives teens a chance to sit quietly, consider their actions, and sort through the barrage of information they receive each day.

Early Adulthood

People in their 20s still often have an abundance of exuberance and energy, making long meditation sits difficult. It is not a time when peo-ple are drawn to self-reflective activity; however, many people in their 20s find that a practice of Hatha yoga—meditation in action—helps focus and concentrate the mind. After the yoga practice, proceed to short sitting meditations of 5, 10, or 15 minutes. Here you can find rest from the perpetual questioning of what life is about, what to do with your life, and whether it is all worth doing anyway. As you examine the true nature of action, you'll come to find your purpose in this lifetime.

As the 20s progress into the 30s, priorities begin to shift. People begin to embrace the life of the householder and to focus on finding balance with family and loved ones. Your Hatha yoga practice continues to show you how to heal your weaknesses, let go of tension, and expand your limitations, while your meditation sits become longer, deeper, and more satisfying. Your relationships grow stronger, your ability to express love, kindness, and generosity increases, but to what degree depends on each individual and your ability to understand the nature of your own reality.

Midlife

Whether you have practiced meditation since a child or have just taken up the practice, there is no guarantee that you will be liberated or ac-hieve enlightenment. Many of you will strive for that as a goal, as if it were something that can be acquired with just perseverance and practice. Yes, these *can* get you there, but they don't necessarily mean you *will* get there, as you will begin to realize as you enter your 40s and 50s. This is the period when you begin to question, more deeply, the purpose of your life. Looking back on the years of your youth, you consider the time wasted, the opportunities missed, the love put aside for career or adventure. You also see the bloom on the rose fading away, your body changing, and your skin telling the story of your pleasures and pains.

Don't ignore this call to go inward, to explore the nature of consciousness. Rather than opt for a more vigorous aerobic activity such as the popular power-style yogas, begin to lengthen your practice of sitting meditation. Although you must continue to exercise, keep in mind that activities that once energized and strengthened your body can now deplete and exhaust your vital resources. Now is a good time to take retreats away from stress and responsibility, to practice mindfulness in your meditation, and to become more conscious of how it manifests in your daily life.

Later Years

The 60s and beyond was once considered a time to retire from the world, to wait for old age and, eventually, death to overtake you. Today, with more people living healthy lives well on into their 80s, these later years can open you to a deeper spiritual practice. As you come closer to the final years of life, there is peace to be made, and days, hours, minutes to be savored.

Many people come to meditation in these later years, as they settle into contemplating their life in more detail and look to simplify their lives. They are more easily able to let go when confronted with their ego's need for control. They see the damage identifying with their ego has caused yet understand why they did it, with all their roles and labels, beliefs, and opinions. Like a skin being shed, they come to the still point of consciousness, and surrender their long-held opinions with less effort than it took to hold tight to the need to be right.

When you observe yourself in meditation, you are the witness to your thoughts and actions. It is not a matter of seeking the Self, for the Self is you at all times. Self-realized yogi, Sri Ramana Maharshi, taught that "There is no reaching the Self. If Self were to be reached, it would mean that the Self is not here and now but that it has yet to be obtained. What is got afresh will also be lost. So it will be impermanent. What is not permanent is not worth striving for. So I say the Self is not reached. You are the Self; you are already That. To recognize this is called 'enlightenment'."

A Spiritual Life

"Some day, after we have mastered the wind, the waves, the tide, and gravity, we shall harness the energies of love. Then, for the second time in the history of the world, man will have discovered fire."

—Pierre Teilhard de Cardin

There are those who know at a young age that they will follow a spiritual path and there are those who come to it later in life. As you have seen from the different stages presented above, a meditation practice can support your spiritual journey at any age. As a young woman Sister Helen Prejean entered the convent to follow her spiritual path.

In 1982, Sr. Prejean became the spiritual advisor to a young man on death row named Patrick Sonnier and eventually walked with him to his execution. A member of the Sisters of St. Joseph of Medaille in Louisiana, she taught seventh and eighth grade English in a small parish school. She never considered that by sending a letter to Patrick her personal and spiritual life would transform in such an explosive way. From this experience, she wrote a Pulitzer Prize-nominated book, saw it made into an Academy Award-winning movie, *Dead Man Walking,* and now travels the world speaking out against the death penalty.

She has found a deeper purpose for her life working with death row inmates, despite the fact that when she contacted Sonnier she had "no special training for being the spiritual advisor to a man condemned to die, no idea where the relationship would take me, and no plan about how to proceed. But God makes a way out of no way. By remaining present to Pat, I learned what to do to help him. I received everything I needed to know about how to be with him, and more."

Sr. Prejean renews herself with meditation, prayer, and contemplation. She says, "Renewal feeds action; it's like the inhalation and exhalation of breathing. Re-energizing and contemplation also happen in the presence of the people that I serve. Some of my deepest spiritual moments occurred when I walked with Patrick Sonnier to his execution."

From an early age, she had made a consistent choice of taking a path with heart. Sr. Prejean is a spiritual warrior. She is one with her path and she knows this from the great peace and pleasure she experiences while traversing its length.

A Man of Knowledge

Carlos Castenada quotes Don Juan as saying, "A man of knowledge chooses a path with a heart and follows it and then he looks and rejoices and laughs and then he sees and knows. He knows that his life will be over altogether too soon. He knows that he, as well as everybody else, is not going anywhere. He knows because he sees. A man of knowledge endeavors and sweats and puffs and if one looks at him he is just like any ordinary man, except that the folly of his life is under control."

To Sr. Prejean, "Spirituality means that the way you live, move, and have your being comes forth out of the depth of Spirit, out of the resonant depths of life, instead of from anything compartmentalized, or mechanistic or cerebral. It's not determined from the outside. It's an inner fire and passion. Jesus said, 'Launch into the deep and you'll have the stars and you'll have the currents of the water which you will learn to read.' We have to move beyond our comfort zone and trust we'll be shown the way."

When you launch your boat out into the sea, you must trust that you will be guided on your way. This is the challenge and purpose you have been given here on Earth: to see past the illusions that you create and to stop clinging to your identity by making the journey inward through the labyrinth of your own thoughts and patterns. There you will find that you are pure consciousness—joyful, happy, and free. When committed to a spiritual practice that includes meditation, you will come to see that the true love you are capable of experiencing lies deep within the core of the human spirit, like a rare jewel awaiting discovery.

Practice

Practicing meditation throughout the changing cycles in one's life can be different for each individual. Its effect on your consciousness has much to do with the amount of time you dedicate to practice. The practices I've included throughout this book can be done by people of almost any age. In the following practices, I focus on teaching children to meditate, although you may adapt them for yourself as well:

- Begin teaching your child to focus and sit by reading stories. Have the child close his or her eyes and listen as you read. Ask the child to repeat the story after you've finished reading it.

- Have the child sit upright in a meditation posture and count the number of breaths up to his or her age, then begin again. This helps children become aware of the importance of their breath and helps to relax and calm their nervous system.

- Turn off all distractions, such as the TV, radio, computer, music, or video games for a certain time period each day. Then have the child eat a snack or lunch in silence, chewing his or her food slowly. Do this along with the child. See which one of you chews the longest before swallowing. This teaches you both to slow down and enjoy your mealtime.

- Light some candles in the child's room at night, turn out the lights, and sit or lay down together watching the candle flame and listening to the sounds of the night.

- Create a special word that only you and your child know. When one of you say this word, both of you close your eyes and listen to the sounds around you. This word directs you and you child into an awareness of the present.

Put a familiar tune to the Children's mantra or say it together when it is time to calm down and relax.

Children's Mantra

Breathing in, Time to be quiet

Breathing out, To watch my breath

Breathing in, To calm my mind.

Breathing out, Closing my eyes

Breathing in, I hear my heart beat

Breathing out, One, two, three, four, five.

We remember childhood songs long after we have grown up, and we often teach them to our own children. Teaching children how to focus and concentrate their attention is the first tool of a successful meditation practice.

Your Karmic Path

It is said that each time we incarnate we do so with a particular purpose, or goal. These purposes may vary from lifetime to lifetime; however, they can determine the type of life situation you enter into, including your parents, family, and community. Our karma determines the physical body we will take, and which culture is the most effective for working out our life's purpose.

Not all lives are the same, nor do they follow the same path, but they can all be supported by a practice of meditation. For example, some lifetimes ...

- Have the purpose of learning to open your heart as a householder. The lessons of love and letting go of the selfish "me" comes from living and interacting with family. Meditation can help you to connect on a deeper level with less blame and more understanding.

- Have the purpose of developing and strengthening the mind with scientific or philosophical thought. The thinker can be drawn away from the external world, feeling cut off and isolated. Meditation brings balance to what is being seen and what is true in the moment.

- Have the purpose of heeding the call for a spiritual life. Meditation opens the aspirant to recognize the Divinity within each human being and lights the path toward finding oneness with God.

- Have the purpose of working out past karma, which may appear filled with tragedy and suffering. Meditation helps the practitioner to understand and live out this karma in the light of God's love.

- Have the purpose of providing joy and happiness to people in the form of music and the fine arts of painting, dance, acting, or sculpting. Meditation supports the way of the artist with insight, mindful awareness, and acceptance for his or her place in the world.

- Have the appearance of being quiet, making little progress in any one direction. In meditation you will come to see that progress cannot be rushed and that and your life's purpose will be carried out whether you know it or not. Spiritual teacher Carolyn Myss says that it is impossible not to fulfill your destiny. It is the reason you are here, living a human experience; your soul will find a way to carry it out.

- Have the purpose of letting your soul continue to grow from good karma developed in previous lifetimes. This pertains to individuals whose lives are filled with love and joy from childhood on. Although they experience pain it never seems to be as tragic as what others experience. They are perceived as having "good luck."

- Have the purpose of a vocation of service to the world, one that requires great compassion and kindness. Mother Theresa was an example of this kind of soul. There are also lives devoid of what one would consider opportunities for "loving helpfulness" and "service." Despite this lack of opportunity, the soul is receiving a life experience that is every bit as necessary as the development of the power to serve and love.

Changing Your Perspective

"The job we have in this life is to search for God and we spend our whole lives avoiding it."

—The Evergreens

In her book, *In Sweet Company: Conversations with Extraordinary Women About Living a Spiritual Life,* Margaret Wolff tells the story of Zainab Salbi's journey towards living her spiritual life out in the world. One evening, in 1993, when Zainab was a student at George Mason University in Fairfax, Virginia, she saw a news report on the rape of 20,000 Bosnian women by Serb soldiers during the ethnic-cleansing wars of the Balkans. As she watched, something shifted in her mind. A feeling of compassion for these women awoke in her. Zainab knew in that moment that she had a moral and spiritual responsibility to help them.

She searched for an organization that served women suffering from the ravages of war, but found nothing quite like what she was looking for. And so she created her own relief organization: Women for Women International. Zainab put aside any plans she had for her future and came to terms with the fact that her life's purpose was greater than satisfying her own needs. Today, Women for Women International serves indigent women in Bosnia, Kosovo, Herzegovina, Rwanda, Nigeria, Bangladesh, Pakistan, and Afghanistan. It serves women who have been displaced by the wars in their countries, and who have lost loved ones, their homes, and any sense of a joyful life they may have once known.

Zainab has an innate understanding of the interconnectedness of all life. She says, "Culture, religion, ethnicity are manmade social constructs that influence our lives, but we are more than these limited constructs. We are one humanity, the human race, and we have a responsibility to help each other regardless of what group we belong to."

Zainab tells the story of a Rwandan woman who lost her six children in a brutal massacre. When the soldiers came, the woman was in church with her children. The soldiers fired their rifles, killing all six children, who fell on the woman as they died. Entering the church to execute any survivors, the soldiers assumed she was dead and passed her by. At the time, this woman was pregnant, and following the massacre she made her way to another town where she had her baby. She also adopted five children who had been orphaned in a similar massacre. Taking these children under her wing helped to give meaning to her loss and purpose to her life.

In a world torn by violence and death, the sanctity of life is evident in the smallest act of compassion. In a culture where our every need is met and met again, finding purpose and meaning in life comes from clearing away our selfish concepts of living only for ourselves. Instead, we must broaden our vision to take in the suffering and joy of the whole world.

Although we often think of ourselves as separate from others "99.9 percent of the 3.1 billion nucleotides (in the human genome) are identical between any two people anywhere in the world," according to Georgia Dunston, director of the National Human Genome Center at Howard University. We are bound together whether we choose to be or not. In meditation, when your mind is silent, when all your thoughts, feelings, perceptions, and memories with which you habitually identify have fallen away, then what remains is the essence of Self, the pure subject without an object.

What you will then find is not a sense of "I am this" or "I am that" but just "I am." Pure consciousness without the small self. It is in this state that you become aware of your connection to all that exists.

The tension that is locked into your mind and body from just trying to survive each day begins to dissipate and fall away, the truth is revealed, and you become aware that what is important is happening right now in the infinite space of the present.

Practice

Sit quietly in meditation. Have your meditation journal at hand to record any insights that may arise. Try to do this at the end of your practice so as not to interrupt your meditation. When the mind is calm, ask yourself the following questions:

> Looking back over your life, what do you consider to be your life's purpose?
>
> Overall, what is the direction your life has taken?
>
> What are the primary lessons your vocation has to teach you?
>
> What are the lessons your family life has to teach you?
>
> What kind of influence does the group you are a part of play on your outer and inner life?

It is not necessary to answer all five of these questions in one sitting. I suggest you take one at a time over the course of days or weeks, say it to yourself before going to sleep at night and again before you meditate. Then let it go, give it no conscious thought. Your mind will take it within, and in moments of silence the answers you seek will arise. Use the Life mantra during meditation to help clear your mind and focus on the question to be asked.

Life Mantra

> *Breathing in,* I see clearly
>
> *Breathing out,* The purpose of my life.

Clearing your mind allows you to remove any preconceived ideas of what you might think your life purpose is all about. Our society dictates achievement by how much money you earn, how big your house is, how expensive your car is. It's easy to get caught up in this mental frenzy. Once you clear away all the extraneous information, with the help of your meditation practice, you will see the truth clearly.

Your Place In The World

"The frightening nature of knowledge leaves one no alternative but to become a warrior."
—Carlos Castenada, *A Separate Reality*

Although we all differ vastly in our makeup, our connection through the web of life brings each of us back to our inner awakening to God's presence. If you do not believe in God or in the traditional religion-based image of God, then you will see consciousness as your higher Self—your better half, as it were. Regardless of your beliefs, know that you play an important role in the world as a spiritual being and that you are made up of the conditioned mindsets constructed from all past actions taken by you and interconnected to all past actions taken throughout time by other human beings. Cause and effect, action and reaction are all part of the connection we have to all that exists in the present and all that happened in the past.

Consider the following few things when meditating on your place in this world:

- Meditation should be practiced with the commitment to enhance the purpose of your life, not to detract from it.
- Meditation should be practiced to strengthen your life's purpose, allowing you to manifest this purpose with clarity and discernment.
- Meditation should not be used as an escape from life, but as a means of making a deeper inquiry into the purpose of existence.
- Meditation should not be used to daydream and fantasize, over-stimulating the mind and leading one away from mindful awareness.
- Meditation allows you to see the bigger picture when casting your life out in the world.
- Meditation shows you that wherever you are right now is the place that is the point of true learning.
- Meditation helps you to see your illusions for the misleading fantasies that they are and dissolve them in the light of this understanding.

- Meditation reveals that there is no escape to be found in a nonexistent future and the pain and failures of the past.

- Meditation gives you the opportunity to manifest your highest state of consciousness.

You'll recall from Chapter 1 that the second limb on Patanjali's eight-limb path of yoga are the five *niyamas,* or life observances, and they concern your behavior toward yourself, how you live your life, and the quality of your meditation and yoga practice. The niyamas are as follows:

- **Commitment** (*saucha*) is necessary when dedicating your energy and attention to meditation. This total commitment brings purity and right intention to your practice.

- **Contentment** (*santosha*) is required so as to dispel all doubt or anxiety from your practice. This allows for a willingness to come to the cushion each day to meditate.

- **Passion** (*tapas*) provides a burning enthusiasm and discipline, which fires your commitment and maintains your contentment when faced with the difficulties of practice.

- **Self-study** (*svadhyaya*) is the very heart of your practice. Self-enquiry is the motivation to undertake the practice of meditation.

- **Devotion to God** (*ishvara pranidhana*) is the soul of your practice. Whether it is taken on with a belief in a divine entity or for the sanctity of all existence, devotion and surrender to this higher purpose raises your practice above the petty concerns of your ego.

The beauty of meditation lies in its simplicity. Doing your practice with commitment, contended willingness, and enthusiasm for the purpose of self-study and devotion to God or the sanctity of life will enrich and guide your practice over the many years of your life.

Spiritual Challenges

One thing you can depend on in life is that it will give you an abundance of lessons you need to learn. Through mindful observation, you can begin to identify the patterns in your life that have yielded specific teachings. For instance, your meditation practice will help you to see how being prideful and arrogant yields a lesson in humility and modesty. Sometimes you might think you have learned a lesson and it will show up again, and maybe even again, just in case you didn't get it the first few times. Perhaps some of the following lessons are familiar to you:

- Repeatedly attracted to the "wrong" man or woman, people who only cause you pain over and over again
- Waiting until the last minute to complete a task
- Saving money for your future and spending it on nothing very important
- Trying to please someone you think is important while neglecting the people you love
- Fantasizing about the future and doing nothing in the present to see that you get where you want to go

Repeat as Needed

In your meditation journal, write down the lessons you remember having to repeat in your lifetime. Notice if you were aware of them only after they had been completed or whether you were able to see what was happening in the moment.

Ultimately your life's purpose is to become a more compassionate and loving human being, and all the lessons along the way lead you there one step at a time. However, it is important to discriminate between the general life lessons and specific life challenges that call you to a much deeper level—in other words, the bigger picture. You may find yourself ...

- In an office of people whose lives are transformed by your patience and understanding.
- Teaching children with special needs who could not engage fully in life without your help.
- Confronted with a threat to your community that calls on you to put your interests aside and take a stand.
- Working three jobs to support your family so that they can better their lives through education.

As I hope you're beginning to see, the big picture is often about self-less action to do something good, something that gives back to the world. However, it can also be a quiet contemplative life, one of solitude and study that fulfills your destiny. You will come to discover all of this the longer you practice meditation.

Practice

Questions can feel threatening or troublesome at times, but they can also open places in your mind, revealing answers that move you forward in your life. Take one of the following questions on any given day. Write it down in your meditation journal, and then go over it in your mind before going to sleep and again before you meditate. Record your answers as the silence reveals them to you.

What is the major challenge facing me in my daily life?

Is this challenge primarily physical? Emotional? Mental?

What is my daily life attempting to teach me?

What do I need to do to resolve this project?

How can I resolve this project in such a way that my life's purpose is worked out?

How can my life's purpose be utilized to solve this life challenge?

Using the word "project" rather than "problem," let's see that all situations are lessons that change with the movement of time. We have but to look at them in the light of mindful scrutiny and they dissolve, leaving us the insights we need to better absorb the lesson.

Spiritual Mantra

Breathing in, My path is open.

Breathing out, I travel free and open.

The purpose of self-enquiry is to bring about change where we have been blocked from moving forward in our lives. You might have to revisit these questions several times over the course of days or weeks before arriving at an answer that resonates with some inner truth. All that is necessary is to sit in meditation and let the practice transform your mind.

Moving Meditation: Confronting Your Life

When confronted with understanding your life's purpose, sometimes it is necessary to hear yourself speak your thoughts aloud. Sit in a meditative posture facing a blank wall and begin to speak, carrying on a dialogue with yourself. If you find that there are two voices expressing different views, let them both be heard. Be careful not to let the conversation digress or wander away from the original thought. Regardless of what comes up, let it arise, be heard, and move away.

When you feel that you have exhausted the subject for the moment, recite the Confrontation mantra to bring you back to the stillness of meditation.

Confrontation Mantra

> *Breathing in,* My nature is absolute peace.
> *Breathing out,* I have the peace of Spirit within.

This dialogue with yourself may awaken things that you could never verbally express about your life. Try doing this practice for 5, or even 10, days in a row until you feel complete in letting go of your thoughts.

Guided Meditation: Following the Tao (The Way)

When you are feeling overwhelmed with trying to figure out the right direction to take in life, or there are just to many choices you could make, take a moment and write them down in your meditation journal. This helps you to sort them out and see them more clearly by putting them on paper.

1. In your meditation journal, write down all the things you feel that you are good at and all the things you love to do. Be as honest as you can with yourself.

2. On another page, write down exactly how you would like to see your life if you could create it any way that you want.

3. Without any judgment or negative criticism, look at what you've written. Put the journal aside and sit in silence on a cushion or straight-backed chair.

4. Quiet the mind and observe the flow of your breath. Let the realization of what you have written rise and fall with your thoughts, just letting it come up and pass away.

5. Recite the Tao mantra to keep you focused, and then let it go as well.

Tao Mantra

Breathing in, I dissolve all illusion.

Breathing out, I dissolve all attachment to outcome.

Our life's path is the accumulation of all other beings' purpose and actions feeding in and out of our lives via the universal matrix of energy. Be patient with your journey toward finding peace with this lifetime you have chosen. When you have grasped the nature of your reality, treat yourself and others with compassion, generosity, and loving kindness. Share what you have learned with your friends and teach your children so that they may begin to understand the cause of suffering and eventually we can all effect peace in the world.

Appendix A

Glossary

ahimsa To do no harm; sensitivity. The first limb of the eight-limb path.

asana Hatha yoga postures. The third limb of the eight-limb path.

Ashtanga yoga: Patanjali's eight limb path of yoga. Is also the commercial name for a particular style of yoga taught by Shri K. Pattabhi Jois of Mysore, India.

Bodhisattva An enlightened being who vows out of compassion to live among the unenlightened to assist them in their journey toward realization.

Buddha The awakened one.

causal body The realm of pure, formless consciousness. Also refers to the most subtle covering of the soul, the anandamaya kosha, which is made up of bliss.

dharana Concentration that leads to meditation. The sixth limb of the eight-limb path.

dhyana Full state of meditation; single, pointed focus on one object. The seventh limb of the eight-limb path.

dukha   Suffering.

ego   The center of our conscious rational life.

enlightenment   Liberation from individualization; oneness with the Divine Source.

Hatha yoga   *Ha* means sun; *tha* means moon; *yoga* means to yoke. Hatha yoga is to yoke together the sun and the moon and with the physical body to unite the mind, body and spirit with universal consciousness.

Ishvara pranidhana   Devotion to God.

karma   Any action: thought, word or deed. The Law of Karma is the law of cause and effect: for every action there is a reaction.

mantra   A word or statement that has transcendental power.

maya   Sanskrit term meaning illusion.

mental afflictions   Negative emotions such as anger, hatred, greed, jealousy, pride, and avarice.

nirvana   Ultimate attainment of liberation and samadhi, once we have burned up all old karma and freed ourselves from the wheel of birth, death and rebirth.

Niyama   Observances; The second limb on the eight limb path of yoga. Ways in which the yogi observes his/her actions both in yoga practice and in daily life. They comprise: commitment, contentment, passion, self-inquiry and devotion to God.

santosha   Contentment. One of the observances of niyama.

satya   Honesty. One of the restraints of yama.

saucha   Willing commitment. Also means purity. One of the observances of niyama.

sutra   A thread or stitch on the soul. Also means short, terse teachings.

swadhyaya   Self study. One of the observances of niyama.

tapas   Passion, enthusiasm, discipline. One of the observances of niyama.

wheel of samsara   The birth, death, rebirth cycle of incarnation.

yama   Restrictions. The first of Patanjali's eight limb path of yoga and define the restrictions placed on a yogi's behavior. They comprise: nonharming, honesty, nonstealing, moderation, and generosity.

Appendix B

Meditation Resources

Books

Bartok, Josh. *Daily Wisdom: 365 Buddhist Inspirations.* Boston: Wisdom Publications, 2001.

Blum, Ralph. *The Book of Runes.* New York: Oracle Books, St. Martin's Press, 1982.

Byron, Thomas. *The Dhammapada.* New York: Bell Tower, 1976.

Cameron, Julia. *The Artist's Way.* New York: Putnam, 1992.

Chah, Ajahn. *Food for the Heart.* Boston: Wisdom Publications, 2002.

Chodron, Pema. *The Places That Scare You*. Boston: Shambhala, 2002.

———. *Start Where You Are*. Boston: Shambhala, 2001.

———. *When Things Fall Apart*. Boston: Shambhala Publications, 2000.

———. *The Wisdom Of No Escape*. Boston: Shambhala, 2001.

The Dalai Lama. *Essence of the Heart Sutra*. Boston: Wisdom Publications, 2002.

———. *Stages of Meditation*. New York: Snow Lion Publications, 2001.

The Dalai Lama and Howard C. Cutler, M.D. *The Art of Happiness at Work*. New York: Riverhead Books, 2003.

Das, Lama Surya. *Awakening the Buddha Within*. New York: Broadway Books, 1997.

Dass, Ram. *Be Here Now*. Kingsport, TN: Hanuman Foundation, Kingsport Press, 1978.

Della Santina, Peter. *The Tree of Enlightenment*. New Jersey: Yin-Shun Foundation, 1999.

Devereux, Godfrey. *The Elements of Yoga*. London: Thorsons, 2002.

———. *Hatha Yoga: Breath by Breath*. London: Thorsons, 2001.

Dominguez, Joe and Vicki Robin. *Your Money or Your Life*. New York: Penguin Books, 1992.

Feuerstein, Georg. *The Yoga Sutras of Patanjali*. Rochester, VT: Inner Traditions, 1979.

Gannon, Sharon and David Life. *Jivamukti Yoga*. New York: Ballantine Books, 2003.

Godman, David, ed. *Be As You Are: The Teachings of Sri Ramana Maharshi.* New York: Penguin, 1985.

Goldstein, Joseph. *The Experience of Insight.* Boston: Shambala Publications, 1976.

Goldstein, Joseph and Jack Kornfield. *Seeking the Heart of Wisdom: The Path of Insight Meditation.* Boston and London: Shambhala, 1987.

Goswami, Kriyananda. *The Spiritaul Science of Kriya Yoga.* Chicago, Illinois: Temple of Kriya Yoga, 1992.

Greenspan, Miriam. *Healing Through the Dark Emotions.* Boston and London: Shambhala Publications, 2003.

Hay, Louise L. *You Can Heal Your Life.* Carsen, CA: Hay House, Inc., 1984.

Houlder, Kuananda and Dominic Houlder. *Mindfulness and Money.* New York: Broadway Books, 2002.

Jacobson, Leonard. *Bridging Heaven and Earth.* A Conscious Living Publication, 1999.

Johnston, William. *Christian Zen.* New York: Fordham University Press, 1997.

Judith, Anodea. *Eastern Body, Western Mind.* Berkeley, CA: Celestial Arts, 1996.

Kabat-Zinn, Jon. *Wherever You Go There You Are.* New York: Hyperion, 1994.

Kalu, Rinpoche. *The Dharma.* Albany, New York: State University of New York Press, 1986.

Kornfield, Jack. *A Path With Heart.* New York: Bantam Books, 1993.

Krishnamurti, J. *The First & Last Freedom*. San Francisco: Harper, 1954.

Kulananda and Dominic Houlder. *Mindfulness and Money*. New York: Broadway Books, 2002.

Lasater, Judith. *Living Your Yoga: Finding the Spiritual in Everyday Life*. Berkeley, California: Rodmell Press, 2000.

Menter, Marcia. *The Office Sutras*. Boston: Red Wheel, 2003.

Merrill, Roger A. and Rebecca R. Merrill. *Life Matters*. New York: McGraw-Hill, 2003.

Ohsawa, George. *Macrobiotics, The Way of Healing*. Oroville, California: George Ohsawa Macrobiotic Foundation (1511 Robinson St., Oroville, CA 95965), 1981.

Osho. *The Everyday Meditator*. Boston: Charles E. Tuttle Co., Inc., 1993.

Ponder, Catherine. *The Dynamic Laws of Prosperity*. California: DeVorss and Company, 1962.

Prakash, Prem. *The Yoga of Spiritual Devotion*. Rochester, VT: Inner Traditions, 1998.

Richo, David. *How to Be an Adult in Relationships: The Five Keys to Mindful Loving*. Boston and London: Shambhala, 2002.

Rinpoche, Sogyal. *The Tibetan Book of Living and Dying*. San Francisco: Harper SanFrancisco, 1992.

Robbins, John. *Diet for A New America*. Tiburon, CA: J.J. Kramer, 1998.

Rowe, Martin, ed. *The Way of Compassion*. New York: Stealth Technologies, 1999.

Satchidananda, Swami. *The Yoga Sutras of Patanjali.* Buckingham, VA: Integral Yoga Publications, 1978.

Shantideva. *A Guide to the Bodhisattva's Way of Life (Bodhicaryavatara).* Translated by Stephen Batchelor. Dharamsala: Library of Tibetan Works and Archives, 1979.

Sogyal, Rinpoche. *The Tibetan Book of Living and Dying.* New York: HarperCollins, 1993.

Suzuki, Shunryu. *Zen Mind, Beginners Mind.* New York: Wheatherhill, 1973.

Thich Nhat Hanh. *Being Peace.* Berkeley: Parallax Press, 1987.

———. *The Miracle of Mindfulness.* Boston: Beacon Press, 1976.

———. *Old Path, White Clouds.* Berkeley: Parallax Press, 1991.

Thurman, Robert. *Inner Revolution: Life, Liberty, and the Pursuit of Real Happiness.* New York: Riverhead Books, 1998.

Tolle, Eckhart. *The Power of Now: A Guide to Spiritual Enlightenment.* California: New World Library, 1999.

———. *Practicing the Power of Now.* California: New World Library, 1999.

The Twelfth Tai Situpa. *Relative World, Ultimate Mind.* Boston and London: Shambhala, 1992.

Watts, Alan. *Become What You Are.* Boston: Shambhala, 2003.

Wolff, Margaret. *In Sweet Company: Conversations with Extraordinary Women About Living a Spiritual Life.* San Diego, California: Margaret Wolff Unlimited, 2002.

Yogananda, Paramanhamsa. *Autobiography of a Yogi.* Los Angeles: Self Realization Fellowship (3880 San Rafael Avenue, Los Angeles, CA 90065), 1946.

Organizations

B.K.S. Iyengar Yoga National Association
1420 Hawthorn Avenue
Boulder, CO 80304
1-800-889-YOGA
www.iyengaryoga.org

Dharma Seed
Insight Meditation Society
Pleasant Street
Barre, MA 01005

The Expanding Light
14618 Tyler Foote Road
Nevada City, CA 95959
1-800-346-5350
www.expandinglight.org

Himalayan Institute
Honesdale, Pennsylvania
1-800-822-4547 or 570-253-5551
www.himalayaninstitute.org

Impersonal Enlightenment Fellowship
P.O. Box 2360
Lenox, MA 01240
www.wie.org

Kripalu Center for Yoga and Health
P.O. Box 793
Lenox, MA 01240
www.kripalu.org

Meditation For Beginners
PO Box 45
Fairfax, CA 94978
415-451-7133
www.meditationsource.com

Northwest Dharma Association
305 Harrison Street
Seattle, WA 98109
206-441-6811
www.nwdharma.org

Rigpa U.S. National Headquarters
449 Powell Street, Suite 200
San Francisco, CA 94102
415-392-2055
www.rigpa.org

Self-Realization Fellowship
3880 San Rafael Avenue, Department 8W
Los Angeles, CA 9065-3298
323-225-2471
www.yogananda-srf.org

Stress-Reduction Clinic
Center for Mindfulness in Medicine, Health Care, and Society
University of Massachusetts Medical School
419 Belmont Avenue, Second Floor
Worcester, MA 01655
508-856-2656

The Temple of Kriya Yoga
2414 North Kedzie Boulevard
Chicago, IL 60647
www.yogakriya.org

Theravada Buddhist Meditation
IMC-USA
4920 Rose Drive
Westminster, MD 21158
410-346-7889
www.carr.org/~imcusa

The Transcendental Meditation Program
639 Whispering Hills Toad, Suite 704
Boone, NC 28607
www.tm.org

Vipassana Meditation Center
PO Box 24
Shelburne Falls, MA 01370
413-625-2160
www.dhamma.org

The World Community for Christian Meditation
c/o Carla Cooper
National Coordinatior (USA)
3727 Abbeywood
Pearland, TX 77584
281-412-9803
www.wccm.org

Zen Mountain Monastery (New York)
PO Box 197
Mt. Tremper, NY 12457
914-688-2228
www.zen-mtn.org/zmm

Index

The New Age Way
to Get What You Want Out of Life